The Impossible Dilemma

by Oscar Kraines

Is a Jew anyone who professes as David Ben-Gurion insisted? converted to Judaism by other th religious authority considered ε State of Israel? Is it true that Jews everywhere are automatically citizens of the State of Israel? Why is a Jew who becomes an atheist still considered a Jew in the State of Israel, whereas a Jew who embraces another religion is no longer deemed Jewish? Why is an infamous Arab terrorist and enemy of the State of Israel considered a Jew while the granddaughter of David Ben-Gurion was not? Is Israel a theocratic state? These and many other much-asked questions are answered by the author.

Underlying these questions is the dilemma of "Who Is A Jew in the State of Israel?" — an issue which has caused severe political crises in Israel and contributed to Golda Meir's resignation as Prime Minister. In this first comprehensive treatment of the subject in all its political, legal, religious and social aspects, the author describes these crises and critically discusses all the cases and incidents involving "Who Is A Jew?," including the *Brother Daniel, Funk-Schlesinger, Langer, Menashe, Rodnitzi, Shalit, Shik, Staderman.* and *Tamarin* cases.

"Who Is A Jew in the State of Israel?" is a complex subject embracing secular and religious laws on nationality and religion, marriage and divorce, conversion, children of mixed marriages, illegitimacy, "Cohens" marrying divorcees, and the extent of Jewishness of the American Black Israelites, Black Jews from India, Falashas, Karaites and Marranos. In addition to evaluating the various solutions suggested by leading secular and religious thinkers, the author offers his own recommendations and provides the full texts of, and analyzes, Israel's Law of Return, Nationality Law, Marriage and Divorce Laws, and Population Registry Law, thereby enabling the reader to follow the dilemma's development and

About the author...

Dr. Kraines, a leading American authority on public law, taught constitutional and administrative law as well as the political and legal systems of ancient and medieval societies, at New York University from the late 1940's to the early 1970's.

He is the author of such books as *Israel: The Emergence of a New Nation, Congress and the Challenge of Big Government, Government and Politics in Israel, The World and Ideas of Ernst Freund: The Search for General Principles of Legislation and Administrative Law* and many articles on Jewish law, jurists, history, ideas, and institutions.

Dr. Kraines served in New York State's judicial system for ten years. From 1964-1973, he served as Director of the Budget in the New York State Judiciary. He was the Director of Operations and Training in the New York State Executive Department from 1951-1963, and a Fiscal Administrator in the United States War Department from 1945-1950.

Retired, Dr. Kraines is now residing in Miami Beach, Florida and is engaged in writing and works as a consultant.

Bloch Publishing Company, Inc.
915Broadway
New York, N.Y. 10010
SBN -0-8197-0392-3

THE IMPOSSIBLE DILEMMA

CE

Oscar Kraines

THE IMPOSSIBLE DILEMMA: Who Is A Jew In The State of Israel?

BLOCH PUBLISHING COMPANY   New York

Univarsitas
BIBLIOTHECA
Ottaviensis

026434

Copyright © 1976 by
Oscar Kraines
Library of Congress Catalogue Card Number: 76-8321
I.S.B.N. 0-8197-0392-3

KPD

.K725
1976

Contents

Preface

In its Resolution of November 29, 1947 the United Nations
called for the establishment of a "Jewish State." No reference
was made to what the State or its inhabitants would be
called. With the formal proclamation of the "Jewish State"
as the State of Israel on May 14, 1948 the question destined
to become a serious political and legal dilemma was not that
of what to call Jewish or non-Jewish citizens of Israel: they
would be called "Israelis." The question was how to define
who is a Jew for purposes of immigration, marriage, divorce,
and conversion and for purposes of registration of nationality
("le'um" in Hebrew, meaning ethnic affiliation, people or
community) and religion in the national Population Register
and on each person's identity card.

Essentially, the "Who Is A Jew?" question is an Israeli
problem in that it basically involves the application of various Israeli laws passed by the Knesset, Israel's parliament,
such as the Law of Return, Nationality Law, Population
Registry Law, and marriage and divorce laws, and the interpretation of their provisions by Israel's secular and religious
courts. In addition, there are Orthodox religious political

parties in Israel which exert pressure in the Knesset and Government to increase the inclusion of Orthodox rabbinical law ("halachah") in secular legislation. Furthermore, as Israeli law now exists, marriages, divorces and conversions may be performed only by Orthodox rabbis.

As the reader will observe, "Who Is A Jew?" is more aptly the question of "Who Is to Determine Who Is A Jew?" A corollary question is "Who Is A Convert?"; and here, too, the question has become more fittingly "Who Is to Determine Who Is A Convert?" In all the incidents and legal cases which have arisen in Israel in connection with the dilemma of "Who Is A Jew?" the sharp and bitter differences and conflict aroused in Israel reverberated among Jewry abroad.

Despite its many severe problems, Israel has managed to survive and grow; and while the matter of external security unites Israeli Jews, the question of religion and state and particularly "Who Is A Jew?" cases and incidents periodically test that unity. As the *New York Times* reported on September 22, 1971: ". . . there is a real confrontation shaping up between the Orthodox religious leaders and the secular political leaders over the old issues of civil marriage and how a person is to be recognized as a Jew." The predicted confrontation broke out in the fall of 1973 and winter of 1974 on the issue of "Who Is A Jew?" shortly after the Yom Kippur War's cease fires went into effect and while negotiations for disengagement of military forces were being arranged. Effects of the confrontation were sharply felt on Israel's domestic political scene, on the international political level, and among the three major Jewish religious denominations —Orthodox, Conservative and Reform—throughout the world. In fact, the issue of "Who Is A Jew?" emerged as the toughest problem Golda Meir faced in trying to form a coalition Government in March, 1974; and it contributed to the fall of Premier Meir's Government the following month after publication of the report by a special commission of inquiry on who was to blame for the initial reverses in the Yom Kippur War.

The history of the "Who Is A Jew?" question in Israel is now seventeen years old; and its dimensions are broad, embracing the political and legal arenas as well as the religious realm. The purpose of this study is to present this history, its significance, and an evaluation of the many aspects of a dilemma which continues to vex not only political and religious leaders within and outside of Israel but also many legal thinkers, political scientists and sociologists throughout the world.

A few words have been made necessary by the United Nations General Assembly Resolution of November 10, 1975 equating Zionism with racism. A contention of Arab delegates was that Israel's Law of Return was racially discriminatory in that it imposed Israeli citizenship automatically and exclusively on all Jews throughout the world regardless of their present citizenship. The reader will shortly be brought into a detailed discussion of the Law of Return and the Nationality Law and will observe that these laws jointly make automatic Israeli citizenship available only to those Jews who choose to immigrate to and settle in Israel and who do not constitute a danger to the health, security or welfare of Israel. There is no imposition of citizenship; and the process is a voluntary one of applying for and obtaining citizenship.

What the scientific-minded in all communities, including the Arabs and their supporters in the United Nations, know is that neither the Jews nor the Arabs constitute a race. There are members of various races who are Jews and, similarly, there are members of different races who are Arabs. The Law of Return and the Nationality Law have no applicability or relation to race. As for the charge of Jewish exclusivity and the argument that if the Law of Return were rescinded a significant basis of Arab opposition would be removed, defense or rebuttal is irrelevant to this study. However, since the Law of Return is one of the foundations on which "Who Is A Jew?" rests, suffice it is here to consider that Arab opposition is anchored not to the existence of the Law of Return but to the existence of the State of Israel. Elimination of the former will not necessarily guarantee the latter. What are relevant to the Law of Return and the Nationality Law in this volume are nationality (ethnic affiliation), citizenship, religion, marriage, divorce, and conversion. It is to these subject areas that this work is directed.

Introduction: How the "Who Is A Jew?" Question Arose

From the year 70 C. E. when the ancient State of Israel was destroyed by the Romans until the establishment of the modern State of Israel in 1948 the question "Who Is A Jew?" was hardly ever posed.[1] It has become a serious and controversial legal and political matter in the modern State of Israel particularly since 1958.

That "Israeli" and "Jew" are not synonymous may easily be acknowledged, despite the United Nations' reference in its Resolution of November 29, 1947 to the creation of a "Jewish State." Certainly not every citizen of the "Jewish State" could be considered "Jewish." While it is simple to assert that an Israeli is a citizen of Israel whether he is a Jew, Moslem or Christian or otherwise, it is far from simple to define who is a "Jew" eligible for both automatic admission and citizenship respectively under a law passed by Israel's Knesset (parliament) on July 5, 1950 called the "Law of Return" and a law enacted on April 1, 1952 known as the "Nationality Law."[2]

Since the word "Jew" was not originally defined in either law, inevitably two basic questions arose in the legal area:

"Who Is A Jew?" and "Who Is to Determine Who Is A Jew?" During his terms as Prime Minister, David Ben-Gurion, eager for new immigrants to settle in Israel, sought to establish a broad definition which would permit the individual to decide whether he was a Jew by simply regarding and conducting himself as a Jew, by being part of a home considered to be Jewish in spirit and action, and by being willing to accept the responsibilities of Jewish identification. To this definition the Chief Rabbinate of Israel strongly objected. For the latter only the traditional Orthodox religious doctrine and authorities could determine who is a Jew.

The first major crisis involving this question occurred in June, 1958 when the National Religious Party withdrew from the Government because it could not accept the Cabinet's decision on the definition of "Jew" in connection with the issuance of new identity cards to be carried by all citizens of Israel, Jew and non-Jew, for security reasons. The cards bore each person's photograph and listed his or her name, address, age, place of birth, color of eyes and hair, nationality ("le'um") and religion. When regulations were being formulated for use by the registration clerks in issuing the cards, controversy arose over the entry to be made under nationality, which in Hebrew—"le'um"—is defined not as citizenship or in any political sense but as ethnic group, people or nation.

In addition, the registration clerks recorded the same data in the national Population Register maintained by the Ministry of the Interior. Recorded also in the Register were the details of marital status of all citizens and residents of Israel. On March 10, 1958 the registration authorities were instructed by Minister of the Interior Israel Bar Yehuda that any person declaring in good faith that he or she is a Jew would be registered as a Jew under nationality ("le'um") without furnishing any additional proof, and if a married couple declared their children to be Jewish the latter would be registered as Jews in nationality without any other sub-stantiation. Accordingly, Jews would be listed in the Population Register and on their identity cards as Jews under two headings—nationality and religion. Two days later, however, Minister of Religious Affairs Dr. Zerah Wahrhaftig, a leading member of the National Religious Party, announced his opposition to the new regulations.

The clash of the two Cabinet Ministers reflected the deep conflict in the nation over the issue of "Who Is A Jew?" In short time, the political repercussions shook the Government and Prime Minister Ben-Gurion backed down. On June 22, 1958 the Cabinet decided that the entry "Jew" would be made for any person who declared in good faith that he was a Jew and did not belong to any other religion, and also for any children whose parents declared that the children were Jewish and did not belong to any other religion. Although the data on identity cards were not to be binding on either the civil or religious courts, the National Religious Party contended that only the rabbinate had the authority to decide who was a Jew, and that a Jew was defined by rabbinical law as one either born of a Jewish mother or who was formally converted to Judaism by Orthodox rabbinical action. No layman, the Party insisted, could declare himself a Jew merely because he regarded himself as one. Moreover, the new instructions had not explicitly precluded a Jewish father and a non-Jewish mother from declaring that their children were Jews.[3]

On June 24, 1958 a delegation of leaders of the National Religious Party informed Premier Ben-Gurion that the Party could not remain in the Government and accept responsibility for the decision of June 22. The delegation raised the possibility of a person registering as a Jew by nationality and being a Christian by religion. To this the Minister of the Interior replied that existing legislation did not expressly state or imply that religious law would apply in determining a child's nationality ("le'um"), as it did in matters of marriage and divorce. Since the majority of the Cabinet Ministers refused to cancel their decision, the National Religious Party announced on June 25 its formal withdrawal from the Coalition Government. A three-member Cabinet committee was created to negotiate a compromise solution to the controversy. On June 29 and July 2, the Cabinet met and again discussed the matter; and on the latter date it offered an amendment to the regulations which stated that a child of a mixed marriage would be registered as a Jew if both parents declared in good faith that their child was Jewish and was not a member of another religion. To this the National Religious Party still bitterly objected charging it violated Orthodox rabbinical law which held that a child must take the religion of its mother and if the mother was not Jewish the child was considered non-Jewish even if the father was a Jew. The compromise proposal failed to appease the religious bloc, and its two Cabinet members—the Minister of Posts and the Minister of Social Welfare and Religious Affairs resigned, reducing the Government's seats in the 120-member Knesset from 80 to 69.

After announcement of the resignation was made in the Knesset a five-member committee of the Cabinet, representing the five remaining parties in the Coalition, was appointed to negotiate with the National Religious Party in order to reach a compromise and win the Orthodox group back into the Government. As a further conciliatory step, Premier Ben-Gurion wrote to the leader of the National Religious Party, Rabbi Yehudah Leib Maimon, pointing out that the Government had no intention of laying down religious law and did not consider itself authorized to do so. The question which the Cabinet had considered was concerned with who is a Jew by nationality, not who is a Jew by religion. In the meantime the Knesset scheduled debate on the issue for July 8.

Here were focused basic doctrinal aspects of a world-wide

controversy among Jews. It would appear that a citizen of Israel by nationality should have been classified as an "Israeli" regardless of whether he was a Jew, Moslem or Christian. However, the Zionist view and the view of the Orthodox religious groups were that the Jews are a nation as well as a religion. The secular Zionist parties maintained that the state should determine nationality, whereas the Orthodox religious parties insisted that the state should define solely the qualifications for citizenship, but only Orthodox rabbinical authorities may determine who is a Jew, that is who is simultaneously a member of the Jewish religion and nation. That there could be a Jewish nationality separate from a Jewish religion would never be accepted by the Orthodox rabbinical authorities and their political bloc. For the secular Zionists, on the other hand, the question of "Who Is A Jew?" became actually the more basic question of whether the Orthodox religious authorities should have the exclusive power to determine membership in the Jewish nation.[4]

The debate in the Knesset spread over four days and revealed how deeply divided the secular and religious parties were. A motion of non-confidence, introduced by Herut Party and supported by all the opposition parties and the National Religious Party, was defeated by a vote of 60 to 40. Before the vote was taken, Premier Ben-Gurion reported on the tense Middle East situation resulting from the revolt in Iraq the previous day and announced that the Government had decided to appoint a special Cabinet committee consisting of the Prime Minister, the Minister of Justice and the Minister of the Interior to examine the whole question and to formulate rules for the registration of children of mixed marriages whose parents wished to register them as Jews. Until the committee would make its report and the Cabinet would take action on it, the original regulations which led to the resignation of the religious bloc's Ministers would not be regarded as in force.

What was extraordinary in the Cabinet's decision was that

the committee was charged with the task of hearing "the opinion of Jewish sages in Israel and abroad on this question, and shall formulate registration rules, which will be in keeping both with the accepted tradition in all circles of Jewry, including all trends, both Orthodox and non-Orthodox, and with the special conditions prevailing in Israel as a sovereign Jewish State in which freedom of conscience and religion are assured, and as a center for the ingathering of the exiles."[5] Accordingly, on October 27, 1958 Premier Ben-Gurion wrote to forty-five prominent Jewish scholars, religious leaders and legal philosophers throughout the world asking their opinion on the question of registration of children born in Israel of mixed marriages whose parents wish to register them as Jews.[6] This request, unique in modern political history, presented to intellectuals outside of a nation, a controversial issue facing a Government and asked for their advice in solving the problem.

The letter assumed the necessity for identity cards in view of the grave and constant danger of infiltrators from hostile neighboring countries.[7] It pointed out that, although the laws of the State of Israel forbade discrimination on grounds of differences in color, nationality, race and sex, it was necessary to register people by nationality ("le'um") since it established the basis for the right of every Jew to immigrate to Israel by virtue of being a Jew; and further, it was necessary to register people by religion since such matters of status as marriage and divorce were under the authority of the various religious courts, Jewish, Moslem and Christian. The letter continued:

> The question has arisen how to register under the heading of "Religion" and "Nationality" children born of mixed marriages, when the father is a Jew and the mother is not a Jewess and has not become converted as a Jew. The opinion has been expressed that since the Register is a civil one and does not serve for

religious purposes (the religious authorities are not obliged to be satisfied with it or to rely upon it, and in general they are not prepared to do so), this registration should not be governed by purely religious criteria. Others say that since "Religion" and "Nationality" are inseparable, and since religious allegiance is naturally a religious question, only religious criteria should be followed, both in registering religion and registering nationality.[8]

Premier Ben-Gurion then posed the following specific question:

.... If the mother is non-Jewish and has not been converted, but both she and the father agree that the child shall be Jewish, should it be registered as Jewish on the basis of the expression of the desire of the parents and their declaration in good faith that the child does not belong to another religion, or is any further ceremony of any kind required, in addition to the agreement and the declaration of both parents, for the child to be registered as a Jew?[9]

In answering the question, the letter recipients were asked to keep four considerations in mind: (1) freedom of religion was guaranteed in Israel; (2) Israel required the cooperation and unity of its people, who came from all over the world, from advanced as well as backward countries; (3) there was no danger of the assimilation of Jews among non-Jews in Israel, for even members of mixed marriages were integrated into the Jewish community; and (4) the Jews of Israel felt an identity with the Jews of the rest of the world.

While waiting for the replies, the Cabinet decided on November 23 to appoint Rabbi Ya'acov Moshe Toledano, Chief Rabbi of the Sephardic Communities of Tel Aviv-Jaffa, as Minister of Religious Affairs. Rabbi Toledano, then 78 years old and born in Palestine, was not a member of any political party but belonged to the Sephardic section of Israel which consisted of Jews mainly from Moslem countries. His nomination was probably calculated by Premier Ben-Gurion to weaken the influence of the militantly political rabbis of the European Orthodox Jewish communities and to win the support of the growing Jewish population from North Africa and the Middle East which in the past had voted for the National Religious Party.

The Cabinet met again on November 30 and announced that all regulations in force relating to the registration of children of mixed marriages had been rescinded, and that the Cabinet would reconsider the question after its special committee would study and report on the replies of the Jewish scholars throughout the world on the subject.[10] On December 1 Herut and the National Religious Party introduced non-confidence motions in the Knesset in attempts to oust Premier Ben-Gurion's Government on the grounds that the Prime Minister, through his secretary, had accused the Chief Rabbi of Israel of "maliciously misleading" the public in connection with the identity card issue. The motions were defeated by a single vote of 30 to 68.[11]

Next the Knesset considered Rabbi Toledano's nomination, and while the debate was in progress the National Religious Party and the Council of the Chief Rabbinate tried to persuade the Rabbi to refuse the post of Minister of Religious Affairs. These Orthodox members of the Knesset severely criticized him for consenting to join a Government which had rejected Orthodox religious doctrine and whose Prime Minister had questioned the status and authority of the Chief Rabbinate on this matter during the Knesset debate. Rabbi Toledano, himself Orthodox, defended his decision and asserted that his participation in the Government might lead to a solution of the registration issue and remedy the neglect of the Sephardic communities in Israel by the dominant European Orthodox elements.

After the heated debate ended, the appointment of Rabbi Toledano as Minister of Religious Affairs was approved by the Knesset on December 3, 1958. The dispute had lasted five months, during which time the post of Minister of Religious Affairs remained vacant in effect, although nominally occupied by the Prime Minister. This was the first time that there was no representation of a religious political party in a Cabinet and also that a Minister of Religious Affairs was designated who was not a member of a religious party. The following July 29, Premier Ben-Gurion, courting the National Religious Party in the election campaign, announced in the Knesset that the question of "Who Is A Jew?" could be removed from the political arena by arranging to register nationals in conformity with religious law and, until a later decision is made, no entries would be made regarding nationality and religion of children of mixed marriages. The resulting agreement among the four Coalition parties, including the National Religious Party, provided for shelving the question of "Who Is A Jew?"[12] The shelf remained intact for three years until broken by the *Brother Daniel* case, which is later discussed in detail.

It will be seen that the question of "Who Is A Jew?" has come before the secular courts because the interpretation of secular statutes is involved, such as the Law of Return, Nationality Law and Population Registry Law, and also because the interpretation of mixed secular and religious statutes is at issue, such as the laws regarding marriage and divorce. Besides the matter of interpretation, there has persisted the aspect of jurisdiction: whether the secular or religious courts have jurisdiction. The fact that Orthodox religious law ("halachah") underlay most of the legal cases and incidents in the question of "Who Is A Jew?" did not prevent the secular courts from assuming jurisdiction.[13]

Law of Return

The Law of Return enacted by the Knesset on July 5, 1950 ensured all Jews everywhere the legal right to immigrate to Israel, unless the Minister of Immigration is convinced that the applicant is engaged in an activity directed against the Jewish people or is likely to endanger the public health or security of the State of Israel.[14] The Law was amended on August 23, 1954 to authorize the Minister of the Interior to implement the Law's provisions and to exclude anyone with a criminal past likely to endanger the public safety.[15] The religious parties opposed the amendment maintaining that every Jew anywhere in the world has the inalienable right to settle in Israel.[16]

Actually, the Law of Return did not grant citizenship to anyone. Citizenship in Israel is acquired by birth, immigration, residence, or naturalization under the Nationality Law, 5712–1952.[17] However, citizenship by immigration is based on the Law of Return, which views Jewish immigrants as returning from exile, but is granted under the Nationality Law with effect from the day of arrival in Israel. Those people, Jews and non-Jews, who settled before statehood—May 14,

1948—were granted citizenship by the Nationality Law with effect from the day of statehood.

In conjunction with the Nationality Law the Law of Return provides Israeli citizenship automatically for approved Jewish immigrants only, unless they formally renounce the automatic grant at the time of entry. Non-Jewish immigrants may acquire Israeli citizenship through naturalization under the Nationality Law which requires a minimum of three years of lawful residence in Israel. Until 1970 the Law of Return did not define who was a Jew. However, on March 10, 1970 the Knesset amended the Law of Return as a result of the *Shalit* case, which is discussed later, and provided: "For the purposes of this Law, 'Jew' means a person who was born of a Jewish mother or has become converted to Judaism and who is not a member of another religion."[18]

While mixed marriage couples are permitted to immigrate to Israel, the Law of Return applies only to the Jewish partner, permitting him or her automatic citizenship under the Nationality Law; and the other partner will not be considered a Jew until conversion has been completed. With regard to converts to Judaism who were converted outside of Israel and who apply for entry under the Law of Return, the latter Law does not explicity restrict conversion to the Orthodox Jewish religious procedure. It was so deliberately written by the Knesset to avoid conflicts with immigrants who converted abroad in accordance with Conservative and Reform Jewish religious procedures. The problem faced by such converts, however, is not one of entry into Israel or the granting of automatic citizenship in connection with the Law of Return and the Nationality Law, but is that of their nationality and religion registrations in the Population Register and on their individual identity cards.

In the summer of 1972 a move was made by the Orthodox religious party bloc in the Knesset to pass a bill amending the Law of Return to restrict conversion explicitly to the Orthodox religious procedure for persons outside of Israel applying for admission under the Law of Return. The bill was defeated. Its provisions and the *Zeidman* case which precipitated the proposed legislation are discussed in a later section.

Marriage and Divorce

Under Israeli law, in matters of marriage and divorce, when both parties are Jews who are citizens or residents of Israel, the Orthodox Jewish religious courts have exclusive jurisdiction. In addition, Israeli law requires that a marriage or divorce between two Jews must be performed according to Jewish Orthodox religious law.[19] In all other matters of personal status, resort may be to either the religious or the secular courts. However, in matters of claims for the maintenance and support of the wife and children, if either the husband or wife applies to the rabbinical courts then the rabbinical courts exercise exclusive jurisdiction.[20]

The rabbinical courts in Israel are Orthodox rabbinical courts supervised by the Orthodox Chief Rabbinate and its Council. The Chief Rabbinate consists of two Chief Rabbis, one for the Ashkenazi Orthodox Jewish community and one for the Sephardic Orthodox Jewish community. The term "Ashkenazi" refers to the Jew from middle and northern Europe as differentiated from the "Sephardi" who is the descendant of the medieval Jews of Spain and Portugal and who settled in countries along the Mediterranean Sea and in the Middle East and Orient. The two Chief Rabbis and ten Associate Rabbis comprise the Chief Rabbinical Council, all members of which are elected for five-year terms by an electoral committee of 125 members, 75 of whom are rabbis chosen from a list submitted by the Chief Rabbinical Council and the Minister of Religious Affairs, and the remaining 50 are laymen elected locally by municipal or religious bodies in various select parts of the country. The Chief Rabbinical Council serves as the Rabbinical Court of Appeals in matters over which the rabbinical courts have jurisdiction.

Marriages between Jews in Israel must be performed only by Orthodox rabbis. Similarly, divorces between Jews in Israel may be effected only by Orthodox rabbis. Second marriages between Jews in Israel are forbidden unless the parties can present valid death certificates for their previous spouses or the Orthodox Jewish divorce document ("geht"). Since civil marriages are forbidden in Israel, Israeli Jewish couples who may be denied Orthodox marriage in Israel and who can afford the travel costs go to Cyprus where they are married in civil ceremony. Such marriages are recognized by Israel. However, marriages between Jews and members of other religions may not be performed by Orthodox rabbis in Israel; and moreover, should a marriage between a Jew and a non-Jew take place abroad in a civil ceremony and if both parties are Israeli citizens, the marriage will be regarded as invalid in Israel. On the other hand, an estimated 1,500 Jewish women in Israel have married Moslem men in Moslem religious ceremony and these marriages are deemed valid since Moslem religious law does not require both partners to be Moslems.[21]

A further complication is the prohibition by Jewish Orthodox religious law of a male "Cohen" marrying a divorcee. Considered a member of the class of priests descended from Moses' brother and first high priest, Aaron, any male bearing the name of "Cohen" or its variations has been forbidden since biblical times from marrying a divorcee.[22]

It is not that Orthodox religious law absolutely does not recognize civil marriage. Under a number of circumstances a civil marriage is acknowledged to be valid. Otherwise, a Jewish couple married civilly abroad would, when settling in Israel, feel and be free to disregard their civil marriage and marry other mates.[23]

In March, 1972 a private member's bill was introduced in the Knesset by Gideon Hausner which would provide for civil marriage in Israel for four groups of Jews who are unable to marry in Israel because of the prohibitions imposed by Orthodox religious law—"Cohens" and divorcees; those born of adulterous unions; widows not granted freedom by their dead childless husband's brother to marry someone else ("chalitza"); and those unable to have children because of impairment of the sexual organs.[24] Proponents of the bill argued that it would not reduce the powers of the Orthodox rabbinate regarding marriage and divorce since it dealt only with Jews whom the rabbinate would not marry or divorce under religious law.[25] However, the result would be to sanction civil marriage in Israel; and this the Orthodox rabbinate and religious parties will not agree to and will put up a bitter struggle to prevent.

In the event that a Jewish couple falls within any of the four restrictive groupings and cannot be married by the Orthodox rabbinate in Israel, the only recourses would be for the couple to marry abroad in a civil ceremony or to be married in Israel privately before two witnesses with the bridegroom giving the bride a ring, both reciting the traditional marriage vows, and the bridegroom signing the marriage contract ("kethubah") and giving it to the bride. The problem then faced by the couple is to have the marriage recorded in the Population Register. Since private marriages are within Orthodox traditional religious law, when a couple so married applies to the Orthodox rabbinate for declaration of their personal status, the rabbinate cannot declare them unmarried and at the same time does not wish to have a "prohibited" marriage recorded in the Population Register. By withholding any declaration the rabbinate forces the couple to turn to the secular Supreme Court of Israel sitting as the High Court of Justice for resolution of the dilemma.

In 1954 when the Supreme Court first took up this matter, it ruled in favor of the aggrieved couple and held that the rabbinate was obliged to declare the marriage valid; but the Court was critical of the need for such a devious method.[26] Gradually, however, the Supreme Court withdrew such criticism and accepted the method as an ironic loophole in Orthodox rabbinical law through which a particular class of prohibited marriages can be validated.[27] This loophole does not apply to all private marriages, only to those which are prohibited by Orthodox religious law.[28] The Orthodox rabbinate does not like the loophole arrangement and has made attempts to discourage its use. In 1970 after five years of delays in the rabbinical courts, a couple married privately petitioned the Supreme Court to require the Orthodox rabbinate to declare their marriage valid and have it recorded in the Population Register. During the five-year interval a child was born to the couple, but the rabbinate insisted that the two witnesses to the private ceremony were not reliable because they were not Sabbath-observing Jews. The Supreme Court did not request the rabbinate to declare the marriage valid but proposed that the marriage be recorded by the registration officials of the Ministry of the Interior in the Population Register. If the two witnesses, the Supreme Court stated, were required to be Sabbath observing then a very large section of Israel's Jewish population would be disqualified from serving as witnesses and might also then be considered to be outside of the Orthodox rabbinate's jurisdiction with regard to personal status.[29]

Apparently, both the Supreme Court and the Orthodox

rabbinate are not happy with the loophole arrangement. The former has frequently insisted that it is the Knesset and not the Court which should be the proper arena for the struggle to amend the laws concerning personal status. This the Knesset has not been politically willing or able to accomplish. Supporters of Hausner's bill pointed out that the Supreme Court has sanctioned civil marriage by the private ceremony loophole arrangement. Furthermore, the bill's proponents asserted, civil marriage for all was not contemplated or intended. Under the bill, the Orthodox rabbis would have the same authority as at present. All couples desiring marriage would have to follow the existing procedure of applying first to the Orthodox rabbinate; and only if the latter refused to perform the marriage the couple would have recourse to a civil ceremony. Opponents of the bill argued that it would create a separate classification of Jews and would lead to ultimate destruction of Orthodox traditional law and control of marriage and divorce. Moreover, the separate categories of those religiously married and those civilly married could lead to greater future conflicts over the status of children born to couples civilly divorced and civilly remarried.

The Hausner bill nearly precipitated a Cabinet crisis. Debate in the Knesset on June 21 occurred after Hausner and the Labor-Mapam Alignment consented not to call for a vote that day. Then on July 18 the vote on the bill was postponed by decision of the Knesset Presidium until after the summer recess which lasted until October. This temporarily resolved the crisis.[30] Interestingly, Premier Golda Meir came out against the bill arguing that she opposed the creation of two kinds of Jewish citizens—one religious, the other non-religious; and she threatened to dissolve the Government if any of the Cabinet parties breached coalition discipline by voting in favor of the Hausner bill. Nevertheless, in her statement on the bill, Premier Meir remarked that "unless the rabbinate found solutions to the problems facing so many couples in Israel she herself would present a bill for civil marriages to apply to all cases, side by side with rabbinical marriage."[31]

It appeared that many, if not most, Israelis felt the solution should come from within the Orthodox rabbinate and electorate, rather than divide the nation and its Jewish citizens into two camps.[32] For this reason a majority of Israelis hoped that Rabbi Shlomo Goren, the liberal Orthodox former chief of army chaplains, would be elected Chief Rabbi of the Ashkenazi Jews and would bring an internal rabbinical solution by liberal interpretation of traditional religious law. One of the leading Israeli jurists, Moshe Silberg, a former Deputy President of the Supreme Court and an Orthodox, observant Jew, contended that Hausner's bill was in full conformance with traditional religious law; and, in fact, the bill would eliminate the need for and resort to private marriage ceremonies.[33]

On October 15, 1972 Rabbi Goren was elected Chief Rabbi of the Ashkenazi Jews, and one of his first moves was to persuade the Independent Liberal Party to postpone its introduction of its limited civil marriage bill for one year.[34] The postponement has gone beyond the one year and appears now to be postponed indefinitely because of an agreement with the National Religious Party in connection with the latter's abstention in the vote on the proposed Lorincz and Kahana amendments to the Law of Return, later described in detail.

While, on the one hand, it may not be politically expedient to press for civil marriage at this time, there is substantial pressure building up against invasions of privacy and family history by the Orthodox rabbinate in its endeavors to ascertain whether one is a Jew under the Law of Return or for purposes of marriage or divorce. Since the key factor is whether the person's mother was a Jew at the time of his or her birth, and since the mother's status as a Jew is determined, in turn, by her own mother being a Jew, the investigation by the Orthodox rabbinical authorities may require a deeply probing genealogical expedition during which personal privacy is sometimes violated by an insensitivity to individual dignity.

Directives of
January 3, 1960

On January 3, 1960 the Ministry of the Interior issued new directives defining who is a Jew for purposes of registration of "nationality" and "religion" in the Population Register. The word "nationality" is a poor and misleading translation of the Hebrew word "le'um" which should be properly translated as ethnic grouping, people or community. It should never be confused with citizenship.

The new directives made "nationality" and "religion" indivisible for Jews in Israel, whereas previously the two classifications had been independent and unrelated to each other. This separation had permitted children of mixed marriages to claim Jewish "nationality" without being converted to Judaism in accordance with Orthodox religious practice, if both parents so desired. Under the new directives no person could be considered a Jew in nationality in Israel unless he or she was born of a Jewish mother or has converted to Judaism; and children whose mothers are not Jewish or had not converted to Judaism when the children were born would have to undergo Orthodox religious conversion if they wanted to be registered as Jews in nationality and religion in Israel.[35]

Registration officials, under the new directives, could not register a person as a Jew in nationality or religion if he or she converted to another religion despite having been born to a Jewish mother. This proviso and a landmark case involving its application are discussed in the following section.

Landmark Cases and Incidents, 1962-1969

Brother Daniel Case, 1962[36]

Oswald Rufeisen was born in Poland in 1922 of Jewish parents and was an ardent Zionist in his youth. Separated from his parents during the German occupation in World War II, he obtained forged documents, posed as a Silesian Christian and was given a job as a police interpreter in the Polish village of Mir. He helped hundreds of Jews and non-Jewish anti-Nazis before he was betrayed to the Germans. Managing to escape he was sheltered in a convent where he lived eighteen months dressed as a nun. In the convent he became interested in Catholic theology, converted to Christianity in 1942, and decided in 1945 to join the Carmelite Order of monks in Poland becoming Brother Daniel, a friar, with the hope of serving the Order in Palestine.

During the Arab-Israel War of 1948–1949, Brother Daniel petitioned the Polish Government to permit him to go to Israel and fight for its independence as "a Zionist" and "a Jewish nationalist." It was not until 1958, after he waived his

Polish citizenship, however, that Poland allowed him to leave to settle in Israel. That year Brother Daniel was admitted to Israel on a travel document issued by Israel to permanent immigrants. In Israel he entered a monastery and requested, with Vatican permission, that he be registered in the Israeli Population Register as being, in his own words, of "Christian religion and Jewish nationality" and that he be granted Israeli citizenship automatically under the Law of Return and the Nationality Law.[37] The Minister of the Interior at the time, Israel Bar Yehuda, who was responsible for administering the immigration and registration laws, informed Brother Daniel that while personally he would like to grant him his wish he could not officially approve the request since the Law of Return and the implementing directives do not authorize such a dichotomy.[38]

After refusing the suggestion of the Minister of the Interior that he apply for Israeli citizenship through regular naturalization procedures, Brother Daniel received permission from his Order's superiors in Rome to take his case to the Israeli courts. On March 13, 1962 he petitioned the Supreme Court of Israel to reverse the decision of the Minister of the Interior and to order the granting of an immigrant's certificate under the Law of Return. The Supreme Court's ruling was expected to make an attempt to answer the question whether Jewish nationality and religion are the same or whether a person can have Jewish nationality without being a Jew in religion. While administrative directives regarding immigration under the Law of Return held that no one who subscribes to a different religion may be registered as a Jew either in nationality or religion, such a view had never been codified in the civil law of the State of Israel.

Appearing before the Supreme Court in brown habit and sandals, the short, bearded Brother Daniel, a member of the Order of Our Lady of Mount Carmel in Haifa, related through his Jewish attorney, Shalom Yaron, the sufferings and ordeals he endured as a Jew and the pride he felt in being Jewish and in the State of Israel. This feeling of deep Jewish consciousness, he stated, still existed in him and was evidenced in his attempts in 1948–1949 to come to Israel and help fight for its independence. He further argued that if an atheist could obtain entrance and citizenship automatically under the Law of Return and the Nationality Law, what is the logic in denying him automatic citizenship when he is proud of his Jewish birth and consciousness? "My religion is Catholic," he maintained, "but my ethnic origin is and always will be Jewish." "I have no other nationality. If I am not a Jew what am I? I did not accept Christianity to leave my people. It added to my Judaism. I feel as a Jew."[39]

The State Attorney, Zvi Bar Niv, countered that a Jew who has converted to another religion is not equal to or better than a Jew who does not observe Jewish religious commandments and traditions. "Jewishness is not a club based on feelings," and being a Jew "connotes not belonging to any other religion." "The attribute of a Jew is a common culture whether you observe it or not."[40] Besides, what Brother Daniel had been and had done before his conversion to Catholicism, Bar Niv argued, was irrelevant. The issue before the Court, he contended, was whether Brother Daniel should be considered a Jew under the Law of Return.

On November 19, 1962 the Supreme Court, by a 4 to 1 majority, handed down its decision. It ruled that a Jew who had voluntarily converted to Christianity cannot be considered a Jew under the Law of Return, and thereby rejected the claim of Brother Daniel that he remained a Jew by nationality when he freely chose to convert to Catholicism. The opinion was delivered by Justice Moshe Silberg, who posed the problem thus: "Once more the question must be asked, what is the ordinary Jewish meaning of the term 'Jew,' and does it include a Jew who has become a Christian?" His reply was: "The answer to this question is, in my opinion, sharp and clear—a Jew who has become a Christian is *not* deemed a 'Jew.' " As for Brother Daniel's contention that non-recognition of his Jewish nationality would mean turning Israel into a theocratic state, Justice Silberg responded: "Israel is not a theocratic state because, as the present case demonstrates, the life of the citizens is regulated by the law and not by religion." ". . . if the *religious* categories of Jewish law applied, the petitioner would indeed be regarded as a Jew."[41]

Here the Court was referring to the religious definition of a Jew as one born of a Jewish mother, circumcised if male, and raised as a Jew. Meeting these requirements, from the viewpoint of Orthodox religious traditionalists, would be sufficient to categorize one as a member of "Ahm Yisroel," a Hebrew term which may be translated as "Jewish people," "Jewish community," or "Jewish nation." Arguing that he met these religious requirements, Brother Daniel insisted he was a member of "Ahm Yisroel." The Court, however, translated "Ahm Yisroel" as "Jewish people" and "Jewish community," rather than "Jewish nation"; and citing scholars on whether Jew and Christian are contradictory terms, Justice Silberg pointed out that while many fine differences and nuances of approach exist among the scholars, all are "unable to regard a convert as belonging to the Jewish people." "The healthy instinct of the people and its will to survive are also responsible for this general axiomatic belief; experience has taught us that converts eventually become wholly deracinated, simply because their children intermarry with other people."[42]

Recognizing there were wide differences of opinion on religious questions in Israel, Justice Silberg stated: ". . . from the extreme orthodox to the total agnostic . . . there is one thing that is shared by *all* Jews who live in Israel (save a mere handful) and that is that we do not cut ourselves off from our historic past nor deny our ancestral heritage. . . . Whether he is religious, non-religious or anti-religious, the Jew living in Israel is bound willingly or unwillingly, by an umbilical cord to historical Judaism from which he draws his language and its idiom, whose festivals are his own to celebrate, and whose great thinkers and spiritual heroes . . . nourish his national pride." That Brother Daniel loved Israel could not be denied, conceded Justice Silberg, but the "absolute inner identification" with Jews and Judaism was lacking. Both simple people and scholars will clearly admit, he concluded, that "Jew" and "Christian" are "contradictory terms."[43]

The Court's primary point was that a person could be born of a Jewish mother, circumcised and confirmed ("bar mitz-vahed") if male, and married in Orthodox religious cere-mony, and yet, if he severs himself from "the historic past" by conversion to another religion, he cannot be considered a Jew under Israeli civil law. It does not matter whether the individual is extremely Orthodox or a complete freethinker, as long as he has not severed himself from the historic past which provides the continuous linkage of Jews to each other as a people or community he will be deemed a Jew. In so deciding, the Court had interpreted who is a Jew in the ordinary sense and under civil law with specific application to the Law of Return. However, the decision did not define who is a Jew with regard to religious law; since the Law of Return is a secular law and its terms were interpreted ac-cording to ordinary meaning, the Court's decision limited its interpretation to secular law.

In a concurring opinion, Supreme Court Justice Moshe Landau expressed sympathy with Brother Daniel's wish to be considered a member of "Ahm Yisroel"; but the question before the Court, he said, was "what did the Legislature intend when it used the term 'Jew' in that Law?" (i.e., the Law of Return). He concluded that for the Jewish people, a Jew who had converted to another religion had excluded himself not only from the Jewish religion but also from the Jewish people and no longer had a place in the Jewish community. It is this idea that permeates the Law of Return; and the Knesset, when using the term "Jew," intended the word in this popular meaning.[44]

Supreme Court Justice Haim Cohen dissented arguing that, in the absence of an objective yardstick laid down by the Knesset in the Law of Return, anyone who declares that he is a Jew and wants to settle in Israel should be granted an immigrant's certificate under the Law of Return and be registered as a Jew in nationality ("le'um"). The requirement that automatic citizenship and registration of Jewish nationality be granted "only to those who profess no religion other than the Jewish faith exceeds in my opinion the powers of the Government." "Had it been desired to limit the application of the Law [of Return] only to Jews not practising any other but the Jewish religion or only those who believe in the God of Israel, or had any other similar religious qualification been intended, the Legislature could and should have said so in clear language. Since it did not do so, the Law must be construed and applied as it stands literally, without attributing to the term 'Jew' any religious significance or qualification."[45] In reaching this conclusion, Justice Cohen on one hand rejected the "historical continuity" doctrine and on the other accepted the view of Orthodox religious traditionalists which holds that once a Jew by birth always a Jew even if an apostate. The curious possibility resulting from such reasoning is "a Catholic Jew"—one who is a Catholic in religion and a Jew in nationality. Truly, this would be an anomaly which many, if not most, Orthodox religious Jews would find repulsive.

Actually, Orthodox religious law is divided on whether a Jew who converts to another religion may still be regarded as a Jew. The Talmudic saying that "a Jew, even though he has sinned, remains a Jew" has been cited by some Orthodox religious scholars as applying even to Jews who have voluntarily converted to other religions. Had Brother Daniel argued that his conversion to Christianity was necessary to save his life he could have been accepted as a Jew under the Law of Return; but he did not so contend and chose to remain a Carmelite friar after World War II ended and after he entered Israel.[46] Since the Supreme Court did not employ Orthodox religious law as the basis for its decision, the anomaly of "a Catholic Jew," and a friar at that, was avoided.[47]

Brother Daniel accepted the Supreme Court's decision as a fair ruling but stated that he still felt he belonged to "the Jewish nation." Although he lost the legal battle for acquiring automatic Israeli citizenship under the Law of Return and registration as a Jew in nationality, he was granted citizenship in August, 1963 after fulfilling the requirements for naturalization under the Nationality Law. The case stirred all Israel and the Jewish communities throughout the world. Israel's secularists, chafing at Orthodox religious control of marriage and divorce and other matters of personal status, tended to support Brother Daniel although with reluctance and uneasiness since the protagonist was a Catholic friar. It had been hoped by both religious and secular Jews in Israel that the Supreme Court would provide a legally binding definition in this case of "Who Is A Jew?"; but the Court did not do so, and instead defined "Who Is *Not* A Jew."[48] As a result, the dilemma continued to vex Israeli society.

Funk-Schlesinger Case, 1963[49]

On December 21, 1961 Henriette Anna Caterina Funk, a Belgian Catholic and resident of Israel, married Israel Schlesinger, an Israeli Jew, in a civil ceremony performed in Cyprus. When they returned to Israel the Ministry of the Interior was willing to grant her status as a permanent resident but refused to register her as married to Schlesinger on the grounds that under Israeli law no legal marriage had occurred. While no civil marriages are permitted in Israel, civil marriages contracted abroad between two Jews are considered valid and will be so registered; but an Israeli Jew marrying a non-Jew in a civil marriage abroad posed a problem.

Henriette Funk-Schlesinger petitioned the Supreme Court to compel the Minister of the Interior to register the marriage as legally contracted. Representing the Ministry of the Interior, State Attorney Zvi Bar Niv argued that the Ministry was not required to recognize a marriage contracted abroad by a citizen of Israel which the citizen would not be permitted to contract legally in Israel. On February 22, 1963 the Supreme Court ruled that the Ministry of the Interior may not question the validity of a civil marriage contracted abroad by parties who were Israeli residents before and after the marriage; consequently, the Minister of the Interior must register Henriette Funk as Mrs. Schlesinger.

In its 4 to 1 decision, the Court did not touch on the validity of the Funk-Schlesinger marriage under Israeli law, but confined itself to the narrow issue of the registration by the Ministry of the Interior. Justice Yoel Sussman, delivering the Court's opinion, stated: "For the purpose of registering the applicant's family status in the Population Register, it is enough that a marriage ceremony took place. Whether this marriage is binding is not the concern of the registration clerk. *Prima facie* proof that such a ceremony took place is sufficient to require the registration clerk to register the fact that it took place." Further, the Court noted: "The law speaks of the marriage of Jews, and only of marriages taking place in Israel. The applicant is not a Jew, and her marriage took place abroad."[50]

In contradistinction to the Orthodox rabbinical courts, Israel's secular courts recognize all marriages contracted outside of Israel as long as the marriages are deemed valid according to the laws of the countries in which they take place. Since the marriage contracted in Cyprus was valid under Cypriot law, the Supreme Court of Israel held that for purposes of registration by the Ministry of the Interior the marriage must be accepted in Israel. This applies to civil marriages in which one party is Jewish as well as both parties being Jews. The question of registering Mrs. Schlesinger's status with regard to nationality and religion was not at issue. She did not request that she be registered as a Jew in nationality or religion.

Ignoring Orthodox religious objections to deeming the Funk-Schlesinger marriage as valid under secular law the Supreme Court ordered the recording of the marriage in the Population Register. However, this did not force the rabbinical authorities to recognize the marriage under religious law. Consequently, if questions arise later regarding the registration of their children's nationality and religion, the children's marriages within Israel, or the parent's divorce, complications could ensue in matters in which religious authority and jurisdiction may prevail.

Matter of the Black Jews from India, 1961–65

Shortly after Israel became a state in May, 1948 about seven thousand members of a Jewish sect called "Bene Israel" ("Children of Israel") emigrated from India to settle in Israel. The sect, then numbering between 25,000 and 30,000 in India, lived in isolation from other Jewish communities for nearly 1,800 years and traces its origins to a number of Hebrew families who had fled ancient Israel before the conquering legions of Antiochus IV, King of Syria, and were shipwrecked near Bombay in the second century B.C.E. In October, 1961 the Chief Rabbinical Council officially recognized the sect's members as "Jews like all others" and removed their long-borne stigma of not being Jews. However, the ruling of the Council extending this rabbinical recognition contained the following requirement: "Suitable clarifications had to be made in every individual case in accordance with directives to be issued."[51]

The promised directives were issued by the Chief Rabbinate in February, 1962 and they included regulations governing the marriage of sect members to other Israeli Jews. Before such a marriage might legally be performed, the Orthodox rabbi selected to conduct the ceremony must "first ascertain whether the mother and mother's mother of the Bene Israel applicant, and as far back as possible, was a Jewess or of families which had married with non-Jews or proselytes and, second, ascertain if the parents of the applicant and their parents as far back as possible had married after divorce or any among them had married kin forbidden by Jewish law. Should the registrar rabbi find that none of the above doubts exist, he will then marry the applicants. Should such doubts arise, the registrar will direct the applicants to the district rabbinical court, which will consider the question, then decide whether the marriage is permissible or not."[52] If the district rabbinical court decides the marriage is not permissible, the applicants may not be legally married anywhere, in or outside of Israel, as long as they remain Israeli citizens.

Reacting sharply to the rabbinical directives, the Bene Israel sect's leaders branded them as discriminatory since other Israeli Jews need only prove that their mothers are Jewish and provide two witnesses. The sect's leaders announced that no sect member would accede to such probes into his personal background. A number of the leaders went so far as to state that the sect might seek the status of a separate community in Israel similar to the Christians, Moslems, and Druzes. Letters were sent to the heads of all political parties represented in Israel's Knesset protesting the rabbinate's directives and appealing for equal rights and treatment as Jews. A private member bill was introduced in the Knesset in December, 1962 formally declaring the sect's members to be full Jews in every respect and forbidding the rabbinate to refuse to perform a marriage between a member of the sect and any other Israeli Jew under penalty of fine and imprisonment.

The bill had little chance of passage; it was defeated by a large majority although much sympathy was expressed for the Bene Israel sect. Opposition to the bill was led by the Minister of Religious Affairs and the Chief Rabbinate on the grounds that: (1) the Knesset would be legislating in a realm belonging exclusively to the rabbinical courts as assigned by law; (2) such a bill was discriminatory and insulting in that it declared one group of Jews to be full Jews and ignored all other Jews; and (3) the rabbinical directives followed traditional religious procedures applicable to all Jews where doubts arise as to Jewish ancestry.

In July, 1963 members of the sect began a passive resistance campaign with demonstrations, picketing and hunger sit-down strikes demanding cancellation of the rabbinical directives or repatriation to India. The following month Zalman Shazar, President of Israel, invited representatives of the sect, the Chief Rabbis and the Minister of Religious Affairs to confer with him on a plan to resolve the conflict. However, the Bene Israel leaders wanted only one action, cancellation of the rabbinical directives of 1962.[53] On August 16, 1964 the Israeli Cabinet, devoting its weekly meeting entirely to the issue of the Bene Israel sect, approved a statement for Prime Minister Levi Eshkol to present to the Knesset the following day at a special session called to consider the problem. The statement led the Knesset to pass a resolution requesting the Orthodox rabbinate to find some way to dispel the feelings held by the Bene Israel sect that its members were discriminated against by the rabbinical directives of 1962.[54] As a result of this action by the Knesset, the Bene Israel sect terminated its demonstrations, picketing and strikes. On August 31, 1964 the Chief Rabbinical Council made a concession to the Bene Israel by agreeing to delete the specific reference to the sect in the 1962 directives. As reworded the directives applied to all Jews when doubts exist about their Jewish antecedents at the time of their marriage application.[55] Thus ended the affair of the Black Jews from India.

Ilana Stern Case, 1965[56]

The *Brother Daniel* case had set in motion what had been predicted by many observers of the Israeli legal scene. In 1965 Ilana Stern requested that the Minister of the Interior change her religious registration from Christian to none, but retain her registration as a Jew in nationality ("le'um"). On her arrival in Israel in 1955 as a minor, Ilana, daughter of a Jewish father and a non-Jewish mother, was registered by her father as Jewish in nationality and Christian in religion. As an adult Ilana became an atheist and wanted her registration in the Population Register to reflect her adult status. The Ministry of the Interior rejected her request; and she applied to the District Court in Jerusalem to order the change as requested.

Ilana Stern's argument was fully in tune with the Supreme Court's decision in the *Brother Daniel* case. She maintained that she had never forfeited her identity with the Jewish community and people by changing to another religion as Brother Daniel had; and moreover, she had never been baptized as a Christian. On June 23, 1965 the Jerusalem District Court issued a declaratory judgment proclaiming that the applicant did not belong to the Christian religion; and on the strength of the District Court's judgment, Ilana Stern's registration as a Christian in religion was deleted and the word "none" was inserted. Under the heading of nationality ("le'um") she was registered as a Jew with the following note added: "Father—Jewish. Mother—uncertain."

The Supreme Court's opinion in the *Brother Daniel* case implying that an atheist who does not sever himself or herself from the historical past of the Jewish people and community would be regarded as a member of "Ahm Yisroel" and would be registered in the Population Register as a Jew in nationality ("le'um") was confirmed by the decision in the *Ilana Stern* case. What Israel's secular courts were clearly saying is that an atheistic Jew is still a Jew; but a Christian Jew or a Moslem Jew could not legally exist in Israel.

Rina Eitani Matter, 1965

By now it is obvious that the Israeli legal arena not only contends with intricate socio-religious problems which try human logic, but also presents ironic complications which test the traditional Jewish attitudes of social justice. One point, for example: Arab terrorists who have Jewish mothers must be considered Jews, while members of Israel's military forces who fight for Israel but have non-Jewish mothers and who themselves have not converted to Judaism are not considered Jews.[57] An interesting matter involving these and other ironic complications occurred in 1965.

Mrs. Rina Eitani, who resided in Israel, was born in Germany, the daughter of a German Protestant mother and a Polish Jewish father. When Hitler came to power, all marriages between Jews and non-Jews and all conversions of Jews to other religions in Germany were invalidated. Rina's mother refused to divorce her husband and chose to follow him to a Polish Jewish ghetto with Rina and another daughter. When the Germans invaded Poland they killed the father and imprisoned the mother and her two daughters as Jews in a concentration camp until the end of World War II. Freed, the mother and daughters traveled across Europe with the aim of settling in Palestine, but were interned eight months by the British in a detention camp in Cyprus. In 1947 with her mother and sister, Rina entered Palestine as an illegal immigrant and resided and worked in a Jewish kibbutz.

After Israel became a state in 1948, Rina served in the youth corps of the Israeli Army during the Arab-Israeli war of 1948–49, and then worked as a pioneer in a dangerous border settlement. In 1959 she married an Israeli Jew, Aryeh Eitani, in an Orthodox religious ceremony performed by a rabbi; and the two children the couple bore were raised as Jews. Her husband was born in Italy, grew up in Hungary, and settled in Israel after liberation from imprisonment in Auschwitz and Dachau.

Active in politics as a member of Mapai Party in her home city of Upper Nazareth, Mrs. Eitani was elected a member of the city council. The city was a new community to which immigrants from many countries were sent to adjust to Israeli life. To help in this adjustment the Absorption Department sent trained and devoted experts to assist and guide the new settlers. Mrs. Eitani was one of these experts.

In 1952, following the first Israeli census, Mrs. Eitani was issued an identity card listing her as Jewish. This was the procedure at that time since there was no nationality law until later that year. In 1961 Mrs. Eitani applied for a passport indicating in her application that she was a citizen of Israel by virtue of the Law of Return. The passport was issued on this basis and was renewed in 1964. Later that year political and religious quarrels in the Upper Nazareth city council, particularly over the issue of religious schools and the matter of the wrecking of a hut that had been used as a synagogue enmeshed Mrs. Eitani in a bitter dispute. Members of Mapai Party were accused by the National Religious Party settlers in the city of wilfully and maliciously wrecking the synagogue. Mrs. Eitani defended Mapai. Retaliating, National Religious Party leaders had discovered that Mrs. Eitani was born of a non-Jewish mother who had never converted to Judaism. Hitting on this sensitive point the National Religious Party maintained that Rina Eitani was not Jewish and had been illegally granted citizenship and a passport.

After investigating her background the Ministry of the Interior ruled that Mrs. Eitani was not a Jew and had received her citizenship under the Law of Return on a false premise. The Ministry stressed, however, that Mrs. Eitani was not being accused of deliberate falsification in her statements. Demanding surrender of the passport the Ministry explained that Mrs. Eitani could apply for citizenship under the naturalization provisions of the Nationality Law which applied to non-Jewish immigrants. Refusing to surrender her passport Mrs. Eitani indicated she would take the matter to the Supreme Court if the Ministry of the Interior did not withdraw its demand.

Reluctant to embarrass the National Religious Party since national elections were scheduled for November, 1965 and Mapai would need the support of the National Religious Party to form a government, Mapai's leadership did not support Mrs. Eitani in her efforts to have herself considered a Jew under the Law of Return. This was sharply revealed in the Knesset on January 27, 1965 when Mapai and the National Religious Party united to defeat an opposition party motion for a debate on Mrs. Eitani's citizenship. Despite this setback Rina Eitani fought on. Refusing to undergo any formal conversion to Judaism, she insisted that Mapai

support her stand, especially since the issue had been provoked by the National Religious Party in an attempt to
embarrass Mapai and win control of or greater representation in the Upper Nazareth city council. Mapai refused and
urged her not to take the issue to the Supreme Court.

After three emergency Cabinet sessions and two stormy
discussions in the Knesset a truce was achieved. In March,
1965 the Ministry of the Interior ruled that Mrs. Eitani's
passport was valid, reasoning that while it had been issued
in error the authorities could not revoke a right granted in
error to an individual if he or she has exercised that right in
good faith. In return, to avoid probable consideration by the
Orthodox rabbinate of her children as non-Jewish, Mrs.
Eitani agreed to undergo a formal but facilitated Orthodox
conversion to Judaism. The matter ended there and was
never taken to the secular courts.

The Eitani incident stirred up bitterness whereas the
Brother Daniel case evoked sympathy and pathos. Ironically
in Germany Mrs. Eitani's mother had been considered a
traitor for marrying a Jew and Rina herself was regarded as
a Jew by the Nazis; but in Israel Rina Eitani was deemed to
be a Christian.[58]

Rina Eitani's difficulty was not an individual, isolated incident. Others have had similar experiences. In the same year,
1965, two other incidents occurred which attracted notice in
the press. One involved a young English Jewish scientist of
outstanding academic achievement who was considering the
acceptance of a position in Israel. After spending six months
studying Hebrew in Israel he accepted an appointment under
the sponsorship of the Israeli Ministry of Defense. Returning
to England he made arrangements for emigrating with his
wife to Israel. Born in Holland his wife had been a Christian
before converting to Judaism under Reform Jewish auspices.
When Israeli immigration authorities learned of the conversion they informed the scientist not to apply for immigration

and citizenship under the Law of Return since his wife would not be considered a Jew unless she underwent Orthodox Jewish conversion, but instead to apply for temporary resident visas which would be valid for three years and at that time the couple could decide what to do. The scientist regarded the situation as humiliating, changed his plans and accepted a position in Holland.[59]

The other incident involved Mrs. Olga Postawski, the wife of a Jewish construction foreman. Mrs. Postawski was born in Poland of Christian parents. During World War II a Polish Jew escaped from a transport taking him to a German gas chamber. At the risk of her life Olga hid him in her house and married him after the war. The two settled in Israel in 1956 and several children were born to the couple. Never having converted to Judaism Olga protested that her children were not registered as Jews and that the rabbinical authorities did not recognize her marriage as valid and would deem her children to be illegitimate offspring of an unrecognized marriage. The problem did not involve the Law of Return since Mrs. Postawski was granted citizenship and its full rights under the naturalization provisions of the Nationality Law. She had never claimed to be Jewish and did not seek conversion to Judaism. Had she converted to Judaism before the children were born then the rabbinical authorities would have deemed her a Jew, married the couple in an Orthodox ceremony, and the children would have been registered as Jews. If the children do not convert to Judaism when they are adults they will not be able to marry Jews in Israel; and if Mrs. Postawski is divorced or widowed and has not converted to Judaism she, too, will not be able to marry a Jew in Israel.[60] As of this writing there is no public indication as to what Mrs. Postawski has decided to do. She has not brought her problem before the secular courts; and there is no disclosure by the rabbinical authorities indicating religious action. Insofar as registration of the Postawski marriage was concerned no problem existed in the civil arena. Following the decision in the *Funk-Schlesinger* case two years earlier, the Ministry of the Interior had to register the Postawski couple as married. The problem was in the religious arena; the rabbinical authorities would not recognize the marriage and would impose the traditional sanctions against the mother and the children concerning matters of personal status. Interestingly, had the Postawskis come to Israel after the 1970 Amendment to the Law of Return, which is discussed in a later section, then Olga Postawski would have automatically acquired Israeli citizenship under the Law of Return as the spouse of a Jewish immigrant, and would not have had to apply for naturalization under the Nationality Law.

Problem of the Supreme Court Justice, 1966

On June 27, 1963 in a lecture in Jerusalem Supreme Court Justice Haim Cohen compared the Orthodox Jewish religious definition of a Jew to Nazi racist laws. His criticism specifically centered on Israel's adherence to the Talmudic law which states that a child of a Jewish mother is a Jew and the child of a non-Jewish mother and a Jewish father will not be considered a Jew unless the child later converts to Judaism. Taken as slanderous to the Jewish religion by the Orthodox elements, these critical remarks were defended by Justice Cohen in a letter to the President of the Supreme Court in which he expressed regret that his statement created the impression of slander, but he did not retract any of his criticism. The letter was conveyed to the Knesset by the Minister of Justice, who said he would not act on the demand by a large number of Orthodox religious Members of the Knesset for disciplinary action against Justice Cohen.[61]

What Justice Cohen particularly decried, and his supporters in the Knesset emphasized, was the failure of Israel to
accept and consider non-Jewish women married to Jews and
other non-Jewish or half-Jewish survivors of Nazi persecu-
tion as full-fledged Jews for all purposes. In reply the Orthodox religious spokesmen insisted that these people could
easily attain full status as Jews by conversion to Judaism.
The controversy gradually dissipated as the Knesset was not
politically eager or willing to legislate any of Justice Cohen's
implied suggestions.

Three years later, however, Justice Cohen again involved
himself in another dispute with the Orthodox religious authorities. On March 23, 1966 in a private ceremony performed in New York City by a Conservative rabbi, Cohen
married Israeli music critic Michal Smoira who had been
divorced from her first husband and was widowed by her
second husband. Orthodox religious law prohibits any male
"Cohen," as a member of the priestly class descended from
Moses' brother Aaron, from marrying a divorcee. This ancient ban was explicitly laid down in the biblical book of
Leviticus.

Since it was not permissible for any rabbi to marry the
couple in Israel and as also there is no civil marriage the
couple went to the United States to be married. On their
return to Israel the rabbinical authorities announced that
they would not recognize the marriage. Justice Cohen insisted that as a marriage contracted outside of Israel it was
a valid marriage and Israel should so regard it; and furthermore his bride was a widow, not a divorcee, when he married
her. The rabbinical authorities countered that subsequent
widowhood does not exempt the divorcee from the ban, and
that from the religious viewpoint the marriage would not be
considered valid. Knowing that in keeping with the *Funk-
Schlesinger* case of 1963 the marriage would have to be registered in the Population Register Justice Cohen adamantly

aimed for religious recognition as well. He contended that
there was no unanimity in Orthodoxy with the principle that
once a divorcee always a divorcee, and that several Orthodox
rabbis had advised him that the marriage was valid from a
religious viewpoint too.[62]

The controversy reached the Knesset which called Minister of Justice Yaakov Shapiro on May 10, 1966 to answer
questions about the marriage. There was no doubt that the
marriage could not legally be performed in Israel, the Minister stated, but Israeli law says nothing about such marriages
performed outside Israel.[63] Moreover, the particular problem
was not new in Israel; it had arisen before in a case in 1954
involving another male named Cohen.[64] The latter Mr. Cohen, an Israeli citizen, applied for a religious marriage to a
divorcee; but the Orthodox rabbinate refused to perform the
marriage. Following the advice of his attorney, Cohen entered into a private marriage contract with the woman in the
presence of the attorney and four witnesses, and then petitioned the civil courts to have the marriage registered by the
Ministry of the Interior. The case reached the Supreme
Court, which ruled that while the marriage procedure followed by the couple could not be condoned the marriage was
valid and had to be recorded in the Population Register. The
development by Cohen's attorney of this loophole in rabbinical control over marriage between Jews within Israel itself so
upset both the secular and religious authorities that the law-
yer was prosecuted and convicted of causing "public mis-
chief."[65]

With regard to Justice Cohen's request, the Supreme
Court could not require religious validation of his marriage.
There was no need to apply to the Supreme Court for secular
recognition; the marriage was recorded in the Population
Register as required under the *Funk-Schlesinger* decision.
Complications in such cases can arise when children are born
to these couples; the children will be deemed illegitimate by

the Orthodox religious authorities and will be unable to marry Jews in Israel other than similarly illegitimate Jews. This matter of illegitimate children of a religiously prohibited marriage is later discussed in detail in connection with the *Langer* case.

The Falasha Wedding Case, 1968[66]

In 1968 the case of a Falasha,[67] Benjamin Gitiye, originally from Ethiopia who had settled in Israel in 1955 and wished to marry an Israeli Jewess who was not a Falasha, came before the Supreme Court. The Orthodox rabbinate refused to perform the marriage since it did not regard the Falashas as Jews. Gitiye contended that his family and social group of Falashas were of ancient Jewish descent and always regarded themselves as Jews. The Orthodox rabbinical authorities, conceding that the Falashas considered themselves Jews and that all males were circumcised, offered a compromise: if the Falashas would undergo ritual immersion, rather than full, formal conversion procedures, they would all be regarded as Jews and Gitiye's marriage would be performed.

Despite general acceptance by the Israeli Falasha community of the rabbinate's abbreviated conversion offer, Gitiye viewed the demand as a personal insult. He showed documents proving that his father had been fully and formally converted to Orthodox Judaism and had been educated at leading Orthodox rabbinical seminaries in Europe after his conversion. The Israeli rabbinate responded that he could not prove his mother had converted to Judaism. Lacking that proof Gitiye would have to convert before the marriage would be performed.

Gitiye applied to the Supreme Court for an order nisi compelling the Chief Rabbinate and the Jerusalem Religious

Council to marry the couple and register the marriage as legally contracted between two Jews. He argued that the marriage registrar in the office of the Chief Rabbinate has no authority to question a person's Jewishness and that his sole duty is to record the proposed marriage and to arrange for publication of the proper notices. If objection is later raised by the rabbinate to the proposed marriage then the question of a party's Jewishness could be considered. The Supreme Court ruled against Gitiye and held that the rabbinate was the competent authority regarding marriage of Jews or of those claiming to be Jews and that it could insist on the qualifications which would ensure that the parties are Jews for purpose of marriage. In this case Gitiye was considered by the rabbinate as not being a Jew and had rejected the rabbinate's technical solution offer of an abbreviated, quick conversion.

The *Gitiye* case differs from the *Funk-Schlesinger* case and Gitiye could not employ the latter in his support. In the *Funk-Schlesinger* case a marriage had been performed in Cyprus which was valid under Cypriot law and therefore the registration officials in the Ministry of the Interior would have to record the marriage in the Population Register. In the *Gitiye* case no marriage had yet occurred; registration of a proposed marriage was requested by Gitiye. In this circumstance the rabbinical authorities could hold up the marriage performance in order to determine whether the applicant was in fact a Jew. Had the marriage already occurred and then the Jewishness of one or both of the parties been doubted by the rabbinate, authority to hear the case would rest in the rabbinical courts which exercise exclusive jurisdiction in matters of marriage and divorce when both parties are Jews or claim to be Jews.[68] Since doubt arose as to Gitiye's Jewishness the proposed marriage was held up by the rabbinate, and since no marriage had been performed Gitiye appropriately applied to the secular Supreme Court for relief.

On the other hand, the secular Supreme Court properly dismissed Gitiye's request for an order to require the rabbinate to perform the proposed marriage and then have the marriage recorded in the Population Register.

Another contention of Gitiye was that if a person declares himself to be a Jew then both the secular and rabbinical authorities should consider him as such. This was the plea raised by Brother Daniel in 1962. Rejecting this contention the Supreme Court held that a petitioner's declaration alone could not serve as the test of being a Jew, but that some objective test had to be applied. In addition, the meaning of "Jew" in matters of marriage and divorce should not be considered the same as in matters of immigration and citizenship.

In the *Gitiye* dispute both sides were too rigid. That the rabbinical authorities offered an "instant" conversion method for resolving the dispute might not be entirely commendable on principle, but its rejection by Gitiye did not call for an award either. As M. Dennis Gouldman of the State Attorney's Department and the Institute for Legislative Research and Comparative Law of the Hebrew University in Jerusalem commented: "It is regrettable that in this, as in other secular-religious conflicts, both sides could not have displayed a better spirit of tolerance and compromise."[69]

The problem was destined to rise again. In 1972 the Chief Rabbi for the Sephardic community in Israel, Ovadia Yosef, stated that the Falashas in Israel were Jews and were descendants of the ancient tribe of Dan, and that he based his decision on the opinions of Israel's first Chief Rabbi, Abraham Isaac Kook, and former Chief Rabbi Yitzhak Herzog.[70] However, the Chief Rabbi of the Ashkenazi community in Israel, Shlomo Goren, expressed grave doubts as to the Falashas being Jews and insisted that any future immigrant from the Falasha community in Ethiopia must undergo full conversion to Judaism.[71] In the fall of 1974 after

Haile Selassie's loss of power, Israel considered offering open immigration visas to the Ethiopian Falashas with special assistance before and after conversion to Judaism in Israel. Apparently, Rabbi Goren's view has prevailed over that of Rabbi Yosef. In any event, because of conditions in Ethiopia Israel expects several hundred Falashas to apply for admission as settlers in the present period.[72]

Matter of the Marranos, 1966–1970

From 1958 to 1966 twenty-eight Spanish Chuetas or "Marranos"[73] from Majorca, whose ancestors were forcibly converted to Catholicism in the Fifteenth Century but who secretly maintained their ties to Judaism, settled in Israel where they expected their return to Judaism to be accepted and welcomed. However, the Orthodox rabbinate refused to recognize them as Jews unless they underwent full, formal conversion. Unwilling to do so all twenty-eight gradually returned to Majorca.[74]

An earlier immigration to Israel of Marranos from the Persian city of Meshed in the early 1950's had found no difficulties since it was proven that they had continually clung to Orthodox Jewish practices despite forced conversion of their ancestors to Islam in 1839. Also, groups of these Persian Marranos had settled in Palestine in the late 1920's and were accepted by the Orthodox rabbinate as full-fledged Jews. Accordingly, all these Marranos were granted citizenship under the Law of Return.[75]

In 1970 a group of eleven families of Marranos from Belgium but originally from Italy settled in Israel. Aware of the experiences of the Majorcan Marranos and realizing they could not prove their adherence to Orthodox practices over the years, these Marranos had undergone full Orthodox conversion in Belgium and therefore were regarded as Jews under the Law of Return when they arrived in Israel.[76]

Shalit Case, 1969[77]

In 1967 Lieutenant Commander Benjamin Shalit, a 34-year-old native-born Israeli naval psychologist married to a French-Scottish Christian originally of British nationality whom he had met while studying in Scotland and who had become an Israeli citizen by naturalization, sought to have the couple's two children registered in the Population Register as Jews. Their marriage, a civil one, was performed in Scotland in 1960; and later the same year Mrs. Shalit settled in Israel. Both mother and father were non-believers insofar as religion was concerned, and Mrs. Shalit would not convert to Judaism. When the couple's first child, a son, was born in Israel in 1964 Shalit filled in the registration application form as follows: Nationality: Jewish; Religion: (no entry). The registration clerk amended the form to read: Nationality: not registered; Religion: Father Jewish, Mother non-Jewish. In 1967 when the second child, a daughter, was born, a different registration clerk following new instructions filled in the form as follows: Nationality: Father Jewish, Mother non-Jewish; Religion: not registered. The latter registration clerk insisted that since the mother was not Jewish he could not register the child as a Jew.

Shalit applied to the Supreme Court to order the Ministry of the Interior to register the couple's both children as "Jews" under Nationality and "without religion" under Religion. What Shalit, in effect, was trying to accomplish was to have the Supreme Court declare that there is a Jewish nationality separate from the Jewish religion. The case came before the Court in 1968. With nine of its ten members sitting, the Court heard the case in two lengthy sessions. The first was devoted to Attorney General Meir Shamgar's presentation, and the second to Shalit's. Shamgar contended that it was primarily religion which defined the criteria for being Jewish, and therefore a person who was not born of a Jewish mother or who had not converted to Judaism could not be registered as a Jew. Shalit, arguing his own case, maintained that the primary criterion for being deemed a Jew was neither that of religion nor of being born to a Jewish mother but was rather that of identification with the Jewish people, community, history, culture and sentiment.

Shamgar cautioned that the issue was more complex and larger than Shalit's personal problem. By ruling in the latter's favor much greater problems, particularly political, could ensue. When asked by the Court whether registering a person as Jewish in nationality ("le'um") signified automatically that the registrant's religion was Jewish, the Attorney General evaded the question by insisting that the issue before the Court was whether the registration clerk in the Ministry of the Interior had made a proper decision within his authority and in accordance with the existing regulation holding that a Jew by religion is automatically a Jew by nationality, and not the converse.

In fact, Shamgar argued, Shalit himself acknowledged the issue's complexity by changing his own registration several times since the age of 13. When he was 13 Shalit registered as "without religion." Later he requested that no entry be made in the space for nationality ("le'um"); and in 1967 he wrote to the Ministry of the Interior stating that he considered himself a Jew by reasons of ethnic group affiliation and education. When his wife became a permanent resident of Israel in 1960 she declared herself to be "without religion" under the heading of Religion and wrote "British" in the space marked Nationality ("le'um"). Shamgar therefore contended that since Mrs. Shalit had registered as British her children could not be Jewish. To this a Supreme Court Justice interjected: "There are British Jews." Another Justice then asked the Attorney General how he would register a child: (1) born in Israel of a non-Jewish mother who died when the child was one month old, and (2) raised as a Jew who later served in the Israeli army and participated in all affairs as a Jew. Shamgar's reply was: "The pragmatic solution for him would be to convert to Judaism."[78]

Shalit maintained that the Ministry of the Interior's refusal to register his children as Jews stemmed improperly from religious reasons rather than properly from secular standards under the secular Population Registry Law.[79] Shamgar conceded that the latter law was not a religious law and that there was no question that the children were by birth Israeli citizens, but he insisted that a child born to a non-Jewish mother could not be deemed a Jew. The generally accepted principle among all sections of Jewry past and present, Shamgar argued, was that maternal descent was the standard test. Shalit countered that his children were being raised as Jews, spoke Hebrew, and were members of the Jewish community and accordingly should be registered as Jews. Furthermore, he insisted, his children had more of a right to be considered Jews than the Al Fatah terrorist, Nimri, who was deemed a Jew because his mother was Jewish.

On January 23, 1970 by a vote of 5 to 4 the Supreme Court, with Justice Yoel Sussman delivering the majority opinion, stated: "The determination of the affiliation of an individual to a given religion or a given nation derives principally from the subjective feeling of the person concerned." Accordingly, religious criteria are not necessarily the determining ones for the purpose of registration of nationality ("le'um"), and the Ministry of the Interior must accept the statement of the person being registered. Justice Sussman further declared that "the issue under discussion does not raise the question of who is a Jew" but rather the question of whether the Ministry of the Interior was required to register the Shalit children as "members of the Jewish nation" under existing population registration laws. The term "Jew" with its many interpretations does not provide any answer to the question of who is a Jew. "All that may be asked is: Who is a Jew for the purpose of a given law?" The laws as drafted, he added, did not intend to circumscribe the individual's right of self-determination, "neither in matters of religion nor of nationality."[80]

Rather than rule on the issue of "Who Is A Jew?" the Court recommended that the Government nullify the law pertaining to the question. "It is in fact a mistake," Justice Sussman remarked, "to think that the matter under consideration requires us to determine who is a Jew." Instead, the Court ruled that the registration clerks in the Ministry of the Interior were not authorized under the Population Registry Law to formulate standards for determining whether or not a person belongs to a certain nationality ("le'um"). In Justice Eliahu M. Manny's words: "In the circumstances of the case . . . the Registration Clerk had no option but to register the nationality of the petitioner's children in accordance with the declaration delivered to him."[81] It was the registration clerk's duty to accept the person's declaration made in good faith unless the declaration was obviously erroneous or fabricated. As Justice Cohen asserted:

> The registration officer may not—acting on his own opinion or that of the Minister of the Interior—register a person's national affinity other than in accordance with the citizen's statement or the national affinity of a child other than in accordance with that of his parent; so long as the registration officer has not obtained the informant's consent or a declaratory judgment of the District Court, it makes no difference that he (the registration officer) believes, or has been directed, that what he wishes

to register is the truth and that the information given him by the citizen is false.[82]

In the Court's opinion the primary purpose of the Population Registry Law, as intended by the Knesset, was population registration and collection of population data. Sec. 40 of the Law specifically stated that registration should not interfere in matters of marriage and divorce, and Sec. 3 provided that the registered population data could not be considered prima facie evidence of the correctness of the entries. As long as a petitioner's statement is given in good faith the registration clerk should accept it and should not refuse to register, for example, the petitioner's children with regard to nationality ("le'um") in accordance with the wishes of the parents.

While the majority Justices restricted themselves to the legal validity of the directives of the Ministry of the Interior and to the scope of the registration clerks' authority, the minority Justices did not so limit themselves and were inclined to tackle the basic issue of whether the child of a Jewish father and a non-Jewish mother could be registered in nationality ("le'um") as a Jew. One of the minority Justices, Moshe Silberg, expressing the traditional Orthodox religious view, remarked that he doubted "a Jewish-Israeli nationality existed" and if it did "it was not necessarily a secular nationality." "The Jewish nationality should not be severed from its religious foundations. The Jewish religious affiliation is necessary for the purpose of the Jewish nationality." "The sole criterion for determining the national identity of the Jew is Halakic (Orthodox religious) criterion which views a Jewish mother or conversion as the exclusive means of identification, and not the criterion which views a person's inclination to the Jewish-Israel culture and values as the means of identification of a national Jew." In short, the minority Justices felt that to ignore or deny the Orthodox religious approach to the case would endanger the unity of the Jewish people within and outside of Israel. Consequently, they rejected any view that would permit the children of a non-Jewish mother to be regarded as Jews unless they would undergo conversion to Judaism.

The decision in the *Brother Daniel* case of 1962 did not hold for the *Shalit* case. In the former, the Court tacitly confirmed a Ministry of Interior directive issued in 1958 which held that a person who declares in good faith he is a Jew and is not a member of any other religion should be registered as a Jew. Since Brother Daniel, though born of a Jewish mother, had converted to Catholicism, the Supreme Court upheld the Ministry's refusal to register him as a Jew in nationality ("le'um"). On the other hand, Shalit was born a Jew and never converted to another religion, but his wife was born and raised as a Christian and never converted to Judaism; and both Shalit and his wife refused to have their children formally convert to Judaism, although the family called itself Jewish and its members participated in Jewish community life.

A new directive in 1960 replaced the one issued in 1958 and provided that a child born to a Jewish father and a non-Jewish mother should be registered in conformity with the mother's religious and ethnic community affiliations. If the parents objected, the child could be registered as belonging to any non-Jewish religious or ethnic group as determined by the parents. If the parents still objected then the child was to be registered only with regard to religion but with no entry as to nationality. The entry under Religion would read: Father Jewish, Mother (the specific non-Jewish religion of the mother) (or simply non-Jewish). As for the space marked Nationality ("le'um"), the space would be left blank.

From the Court majority's reasoning it could be inferred that a person might hold Jewish nationality without belonging to the Jewish religion and that a Jew is anyone who in good faith says he is a Jew. Actually, however, the Court did not generalize any principles, but ruled that in Shalit's case his two children could be registered as Jewish in nationality ("le'um") with no entry regarding religion despite their mother not being a Jew. Further, the Court requested the Attorney General to convey to the Government a recommendation that Sec. Two (B) (6) of the Population Registry Law of 1965 be rescinded and that in the future the Population Register contain details only of an individual's national allegiance and citizenship, but not of his or her nationality ("le'um"). Justice Shimon Agranat, President of the Supreme Court, announced that the Court would defer its decision until it received the Government's response to its recommendation. If the Government rejected the recommendation the Court would then enter into the merits of the case and would decide whether a person could be a Jew by nationality without being Jewish by religion. This was the Court's method for evading a decision on the question of "Who Is A Jew?" and for avoiding the aggravation of the already strained relations between the religious and secular political parties comprising the Coalition Government.

Insofar as the Shalits themselves were concerned they had won their case. They sued to have the children registered as Jews by nationality ("le'um") and of no religion, and the Supreme Court upheld them on the technicality of the registration clerk's authority rather than on the issue of "Who Is A Jew?" The Government was faced with having to consent to register the Shalit children as ordered by the Supreme Court or else defy the nation's highest judicial authority. Accordingly, the Shalit children were registered as Jews in nationality ("le'um") and of no religion. The difficulty facing the two children, however, will arise when as adults they wish to marry a Jewish partner in Israel; they may not be able to do so without formal conversion to Judaism, assuming that civil marriage will continue to be prohibited.

The Court's decision in the *Shalit* case not only restricted its application to the two Shalit children, but confined its effect to the entries in the Population Register. It had no bearing on the laws and regulations pertaining to marriage and divorce. In 1971 a third child was born to the Shalits. While no publicity was given to the new child's registration, the 1970 Amendment to the Law of Return, discussed in the next section, required the registration authorities to decline to register the third child as a Jew.[83] Interestingly, when the *Shalit* case was being considered by the Supreme Court, a Member of the Knesset representing the National Religious Party proposed a bill on July 2, 1969 which would have removed the authority of the secular courts to hear cases on the question of "Who Is A Jew?" and would have assigned such authority exclusively to the Orthodox rabbinical courts. However, the bill never reached the floor of the Knesset.

Commenting on the *Shalit* case in the *Israel Law Review,* Benjamin Akzin, Professor of Constitutional Law and Political Science at the Hebrew University in Jerusalem, remarked: "It is quite plausible that in Israel the link between Jewish nationality and religion will become more tenuous in the course of time. What Mr. Shalit wanted was to have this historical process given an official stamp as a *fait accompli* established by judicial *fiat.* The judges felt, and rightly so in this writer's opinion, that this was hardly a judicial function, that theirs was neither to serve as hindrance to sociological change nor to push society toward such a change before it has clearly manifested readiness for it."[84] Shalit himself said that he thought the Supreme Court had deliberately side-stepped the issue: "I think the judges attached more importance to the formal duty of the registrar than to the question of who is a Jew." The Orthodox religious Jew, Shalit felt, was not prepared to understand, let alone accept the view, that a non-religious person could consider himself as deeply Jewish culturally as a person could regard himself Jewish by virtue of religious beliefs and practices. Nevertheless, Shalit was satisfied with the decision.[85]

1970 Amendment to the Law of Return⁸⁶

The *Shalit* decision stirred the public for days. Newspapers carried discussions on the case, and paid advertisements were inserted praising or protesting the stand of the Orthodox rabbinate and defending or attacking the Shalits. Public meetings were held for each side. The effect of the Supreme Court decision on the Orthodox rabbinate was particularly profound. On January 25, 1970 the National Religious Party announced that it would resign from the Government Coalition unless the Knesset passed legislation reversing the Court's decision.[87] Four days later the Cabinet voted to recommend to the Knesset the legislation demanded by the National Religious Party;[88] and, as reciprocation, the Cabinet requested that the Chief Rabbinate shorten and speed up the conversion process since the existing three-year length for conversion was causing great anguish to many Israeli citizens and their children.[89]

During the debates in the Knesset in February, 1970 on the Cabinet's proposed legislation, a Member of the Knesset tore up his identity card while at the Speaker's rostrum insisting that religion and nationality ("le'um") were private matters and by including such data in the Population Register and on the personal identity cards Israel was doing what Jews had bitterly opposed in other lands for centuries. Another Member ironically pointed out that under the Cabinet's proposals some of David Ben-Gurion's grandchildren would not be considered Jews since his son had married a non-Jew who had not converted, while Nikita S. Khrushchev's grandchildren would be deemed Jews because his son married a Jewish woman.[90] A third Member, an ultra-Orthodox rabbi, spat on a prayer book of the Reform Jewish movement and threw it on the floor. A motion to discipline him was withdrawn after he apologized.[91]

To avoid a Cabinet crisis and a bitter split within the country at a time when war might break out again with the surrounding Arab nations the Cabinet proposed a compromise. It would not initiate legislation to amend the Population Registry Law as recommended by the Supreme Court, but it would order that Shalit's children be registered as Jews by nationality ("le'um") and with no religion. However, to placate the Orthodox religious sections of the public and their representatives in the Knesset and the Cabinet, the Government would propose legislation which would, for registration purposes, define a Jew as "a person born of a Jewish mother or converted to Judaism, who is not a member of another religion." This criterion for registration was strictly in accordance with Orthodox religious law. The compromise called also for the provisions of the Law of Return to be extended to all members of an immigrant family if either one of the parents is Jewish. While this would give Israeli citizenship automatically even to a child of a non-Jewish mother, it would not grant recognition of Jewish nationality ("le'um").[92]

The Cabinet's compromise proposal stirred stormy debate in the Knesset; but it was enacted into law on March 10, 1970 by a vote of 51 to 14, with 9 abstentions. As passed, the law incorporated the provisions of the compromise proposed by the Cabinet but added that a Jew who has converted to another religion has changed not only his religion but also his nationality ("le'um"). Implicit in the new law was the rejection of the secular contention that Jewish religion and nationality ("le'um") are separable. Thus, immigrants of non-Jewish mothers could be given automatic Israeli citizenship but would not be registered as Jews unless they converted to Judaism. Also, the immigrant who is the child of a Jewish mother or of a mother who has converted to Judaism—and if the immigrant is not a member of any other religion—must be registered as a Jew and is entitled to the rights granted under the Law of Return. Another feature of the new law was that it provided for the right of immigration with automatic citizenship to former Jews who left the Jewish religion involuntarily and who are reclaiming their Jewish nationality ("le'um"). Significantly, while the new law incorporated Orthodox religious concepts of who is a Jew, it omitted any mention of traditional Orthodox requirements with regard to conversion to Judaism. This later became the focal point of another conflict between secular and religious elements and also between Orthodox and non-Orthodox Judaism.[93] As for a person who is a member of another religion he will be considered also non-Jewish in nationality ("le'um") despite his or her birth to a Jewish mother or previous conversion to Judaism. The Knesset thus gave statutory recognition to the Supreme Court's decision in the *Brother Daniel* case, and for the first time defined the word "Jew" which had appeared in many Israeli statutes before.

As amended by the above legislation, the Law of Return provided a definition of who is a Jew which did not include any member of a Jewish person's family who was not himself or herself born to a Jewish mother or was not converted to Judaism. To make such an individual eligible for automatic citizenship—not nationality ("le'um")—under the Law of

Return and the Nationality Law, Sec. 1 of the new legislation added a Sec. 4A to the Law of Return which provided that the rights of a Jew under the Law of Return and the rights of an immigrant under the Nationality Law, in addition to the rights enjoyed by an immigrant under all other legislation, shall be extended also to the child or grandchild of a Jew and to his or her spouse and to the spouse of his or her child or grandchild, but not to a person who was a Jew and who voluntarily converted to another religion. Accordingly, the non-Jewish spouses, children and grandchildren of Jewish immigrants would be granted not only automatic citizenship—not nationality ("le'um")—but also similar tax benefits, housing and other privileges provided to new Jewish immigrants.[94]

Whereas the Supreme Court in the *Shalit* case had suggested that the nationality ("le'um") item in the Population Register and on the identity card be eliminated, the Knesset in its legislation of March 10, 1970 amended the Population Registry Law by providing that "no person shall be registered as of Jewish nationality or religion if any statement under this Law or other entry in the register or public document shows that he is not a Jew, unless such statement, ruling or document—as aforesaid—is contradicted to the satisfaction of the Chief Registration Officer or unless it has otherwise been decided by a declaratory judgment of the competent court or tribunal."[95] In general the legislation of March 10, 1970 did not resolve the problem of "Who Is A Jew?" Although on the registration matter the Orthodox rabbinate won out, the victory was not complete; and while the Shalits won a personal victory, the new legislation sealed it as an individual incident which would not thereafter be repeated for others. For those who desire to belong to the Jewish community and be registered as belonging but who reject any religious affiliation and registration, the Supreme Court decision in the *Shalit* case and the Knesset's legisla-

tion of March 10, 1970 provided no broad, satisfactory solution. What the Court had accomplished, however, was to
make a dent with one individual case in the indivisibility of
Jewish nationality and religion, and to force the Knesset to
take a stand and define by legislation for the first time who,
by objective criteria, is a Jew.[96]

Shortly after the *Shalit* decision, Shalev Ginossar, Professor of Law at the Hebrew University of Jerusalem, remarked
in an article in the *Israel Law Review* in April, 1970:

> Despite this, the problem has not been fundamentally solved:
> the test of who is a Jew is still neither objective nor subjective;
> nor is it either purely religious or purely national. Instead of a
> solution, we have been treated to a compromise which is equally
> unpalatable to the doctrinaires on both sides of the fence. The
> secularists resent the concept of Jewish "nationality" being
> defined in terms of religious affiliation; while the religious-
> minded take offence at every departure from strict orthodoxy.
> Even more serious, conversion being at best exceptional, the
> normal line to Judaism derives by heredity from some other
> person whose own origin needs to be traced, and so forth *ad
> infinitum* in an unending chain of pedigree research; and like the
> *probatio diabolica* which so baffled the Scholastics, this is a
> difficulty which cannot be overcome without the help of pre-
> sumptions.[97]

The Amendment to the Law of Return did not specifically
prohibit the recognition by registration authorities of conversions to Judaism abroad by non-Orthodox rabbis. As for
conversions to Judaism performed in Israel, the Amendment
did not apply at all, particularly since an unrepealed ordinance of the British Mandate period assigned such authority
solely to the Orthodox rabbinate. Also, the Amendment did
not affect questions of marriage and divorce.[98] The issues of
conversion abroad and of marriage and divorce gradually

became more aggravating; and by 1974 they contributed to Premier Golda Meir's difficulties in forming a government and ultimately to her resignation and retirement from political office. These issues are discussed in detail later.

Landmark Cases
and Incidents,
1970-1973

Helen Zeidman Matter, *1970*

In June, 1970 the question of "Who Is A Jew?" sharply took on an added dimension, that of conversion to Judaism performed by rabbis who are not Orthodox. Mrs. Helen Zeidman, an American-born Christian, married a Jew and was converted in 1967 to Judaism by three Reform rabbis in Tel Aviv. Three years later she requested that she be registered in the Population Register and on her identity card as a Jew in nationality ("le'um") and religion. The Ministry of the Interior denied the request on the ground that the conversion had not been performed by an Orthodox rabbi; and the Chief Rabbinate insisted it would not consider any conversion valid unless it was Orthodox, regardless whether the conversion took place within or outside of Israel. Mrs. Zeidman applied to the Supreme Court to compel the Minister of the Interior to make the requested entry changes.[99]

Again the National Religious Party threatened to resign from the Coalition Government and began to exert political pressure. In a letter publicly addressed to the Minister of the Interior, the Minister of Justice stated that he had no authority to give any legal opinions on conversions which occurred outside of Israel; but since Mrs. Zeidman was converted in Israel, the refusal of the Minister of the Interior to register her as Jewish was, in his opinion, lawful and he would defend that position before the Supreme Court. In any event, the validity of the marriage was not being questioned.

While the case was before the Supreme Court, the Cabinet decided it would not take a stand on the case but would allow the Minister of the Interior to pursue his arguments on his own. Public opinion appeared to support Mrs. Zeidman and expected the Court to rule in her favor. Angered at the Cabinet's policy, the National Religious Party instructed its three Cabinet members to resign unless the Cabinet would support the Orthodox stand. The Cabinet gave in and applied pressure to have Mrs. Zeidman back down. The day before the Supreme Court was scheduled to hand down its decision, it was announced that Mrs. Zeidman had undergone Orthodox conversion. In disgust her attorney withdrew and the Court made no ruling. Mrs. Zeidman explained that she was distressed by the political repercussions her case had caused and that all she wanted was to insure her children's registration as Jews. Consequently the key issue of conversion to Judaism performed by other than Orthodox rabbis was left unresolved.[100]

I. Ben Menashe Case, 1970[101]

The cases and incidents discussed thus far generally involved requests for positive action—the insertion of entries in the Population Register and identity cards. What of requests for negative action—omissions of entries? In 1970 a case involving negative action came before the Supreme Court. I. Ben Menashe, an Israeli Jewish attorney whose children were registered as Jews in both nationality ("le'um") and religion despite his request that no registration be made at all under both these headings, applied to the Ministry of the Interior to carry out his request. The Ministry agreed to remove only the registration regarding religion. Insisting on the removal of both registrations, Menashe filed suit in the secular courts; and the case went to the Supreme Court.

Following its decision in the *Shalit* case, the Supreme Court upheld Menashe's contention that a person who did not wish to be classified as a Jew by nationality ("le'um") had the right to have such declaration omitted from the Population Register and identity card. Moreover, it was not essential that the nationality ("le'um") of a person appear on the Register or identity card. The laws affecting registration, the Court maintained, spell out only who may *not* be registered as a Jew, and not who must be so registered. Omissions of entries are legal, but positive entries such as Brother Daniel had requested were illegal.[102]

Rodnitzi Case and the Religious Ban on "Cohens" Marrying Divorcees, 1970[103]

The year 1970 was a busy one for the Supreme Court and the "Who Is A Jew?" question. No sooner had the Court disposed of the *Menashe* case when another suit came before it regarding registration of a marriage between a "Cohen" and a divorcee. This case involved a Jewish couple who were married in 1965 in a private ceremony in Israel without the participation of clergy after the Orthodox rabbinate refused to marry them. Reason for the refusal was that the woman was a divorcee and the man was a member of the priestly class of "Cohens" descended from the biblical high priest Aaron. After the private marriage the couple applied to the Orthodox rabbinate to confirm the marriage or define their marital status.

In a similar case in 1963[104] the Orthodox rabbinical courts refused to regard the marriage as valid and directed that neither party could marry anyone else without first obtaining a divorce. This created a logical loophole for recognizing that a marriage had taken place. Since a divorce was required before either party could remarry, the Minister of the Interior was forced to conclude that the couple were not un-attached and therefore had to register them as married. It was on this precedent that the Rodnitzis tried the same strategy. Again the rabbinical courts refused to recognize the marriage but held that they could not remarry unless they first obtained a divorce. After lingering in the rabbinical courts for about five years, the case reached the Supreme Court in 1970 on several grounds, including competency of the civil courts to try such a case. In the meantime a child had been born to the couple.

On June 16, 1970 the Court, by 4 to 1 majority, held first that ordinarily it is the rabbinical courts' authority to rule on the validity of a marriage; but since they had refused to clarify the marital status of the couple other than to insist that they would not recognize the marriage and that the couple could not remarry without first obtaining a divorce, then the civil courts were free to assume competence. As the Supreme Court viewed the case, if there had been no mar-riage how can there be a divorce? If a divorce was required for remarriage then there must have been a marriage. Conse-quently, the Supreme Court ordered the Minister of the Interior to register the couple as legally married. The Court, however, could not upset the ban on remarriage without prior divorce nor could it deny the competence of the rab-binical courts to require the divorce before remarrying.[105]

Zigi Staderman Case, 1970[106]

For political reasons the Knesset, when confronted with the
Orthodox religious opposition to the *Shalit* decision, has-
tened to reverse legislatively the Supreme Court's ruling and
passed the 1970 Amendment to the Law of Return. One
Israeli Jewish citizen, Zigi Staderman, was so incensed at the
Orthodox religious pressure on the Cabinet and Knesset that
he applied to the Minister of the Interior to have the entry
of his Jewish nationality ("le'um") stricken from the Population Register and his identity card. He received no response
from the Ministry, and he then petitioned the Supreme Court
to order the Minister of the Interior to comply with his
application.[107]

Under the Population Registry Law of 1965, changes in
registration were to be accomplished by filing a proper judgment or declaration of court, or by filing a notice accompanied by a public document attesting to or affirming the
change. Both these conditions were absent in this case. Accordingly, the Supreme Court dismissed Staderman's petition, ignoring the petitioner's specific intention of simply
removing the existing registration entry without requesting
substitution of another entry.

In effect, striking out the existing entry and leaving the
nationality ("le'um") line empty would constitute a change
in registration. In the Court's opinion the 1970 Amendment
to the Law of Return aimed not at affecting any existing
registration but at legislatively upsetting the Court's decision
in the *Shalit* case. Staderman openly contended that his
purpose in petitioning the Supreme Court was to protest the
enactment of the 1970 Amendment to the Law of Return.
Nevertheless, while the Supreme Court stated that the 1970
Amendment did not affect existing registrations, it did make
a difference for persons born or settling in Israel after enact-

ment of the Amendment. Those with prior registrations carried forward their existing registrations whether or not they now met the new definition of who is a Jew. Since Staderman did not maintain that he was not Jewish as defined by the 1970 Amendment, and since he was Jewish as defined under either the old or new definition, his petition merely constituted a personal protest and an assertion of a right of self-determination with which, the Court stated, the law was not at all concerned.[108]

Matter of the Karaites, 1961–1971

Israel has a wide variety of Jews from many sections of the world whose cultural backgrounds have little in common with the Jews from Eastern and Western Europe. One of these different groups is the Karaite community in Israel which numbers approximately 8,000, the bulk of whom emigrated mainly from Egypt. Its beliefs are traced back to Babylonia in the Eighth Century C.E. where Anan Ben David and his followers, calling themselves "Karaites" ("Readers of Scripture"), rejected the rabbinical oral law—the Talmud—as had the Sadducees eight hundred years before, and insisted on the exclusivity of the written law—the Old Testament—as the basis of Jewish religious law. In attacking the validity of the oral law, Anan Ben David bitterly opposed the twin pillars of Talmudic authority at the time—the Babylonian academies of Sura and Pumbeditha. As a result, the Karaite movement caused a split in ancient Judaism.

The Karaites grew in the Ninth to Twelfth Centuries, spreading from Babylonia to Palestine, Egypt and Spain. In the Twentieth Century the majority of the Karaites were in the Russian Crimea and Egypt. The Orthodox rabbis today regard the Karaites as Jews but do not approve of marriages between Karaites and other Jews. Neither do the Karaite rabbis permit their members to marry other Jews. Nevertheless in 1969 the Rabbinical Court of Haifa declared legal a marriage between a Karaite and a non-Karaite Jew;[109] and in 1973 Ovadia Yosef, the Chief Rabbi of the Sephardic community in Israel, recognized a Karaite as a full-fledged Jew on the basis of what some Orthodox elements felt was "rather slim testimony."[110] The matter of the Karaites has become more than "Who Is A Jew?"; it is now a question of "How Much of A Jew Is A Karaite?"

Yolanda Gerstel Matter, 1971

On March 30, 1971 Mrs. Yolanda Gerstel, a Catholic married to a Jew, immigrated to Israel with her husband. Both were Belgian nationals prior to their settling in Israel; and while in Belgium Mrs. Gerstel had filled out the proper immigration application forms and indicated that she was a Catholic. When she arrived in Israel the immigration officials registered her as Jewish, but she did not discover the error until two months later.

Reporting the mistake to the Ministry of the Interior, Mrs. Gerstel requested that correction be made. However, the Ministry replied that no change could be made until Mrs. Gerstel produced the proper documents from Belgium certifying her religion to be Catholic. If such documents were not provided then Mrs. Gerstel would have to apply to the Israeli courts for a declaratory judgment stating that she was Catholic and directing the Minister of the Interior to change her registration from Jewish to Catholic. For over a year Mrs. Gerstel followed neither course and chose to let things stand as they were. Accordingly she was regarded as a Jew by virtue of mutual default.[111] In 1972, however, it was reported in an American Jewish newspaper that Mrs. Gerstel in-

tended to undergo Orthodox conversion to Judaism.[112] No
further information was made public thereafter.

George Raphael Tamarin Case, 1972[113]

Dr. George Raphael Tamarin, a psychologist and an avowed
atheist but born a Jew, immigrated to Israel from Yugoslavia
in 1949 and was registered at that time as a Jew by nationality
and of no religion. After enactment of the 1970 Amendment
to the Law of Return, he petitioned the Ministry of the
Interior to change his nationality registration from "Jewish"
to "Israeli" and to continue his registration as an atheist with
regard to religion. The Ministry of the Interior rejected his
request. Dr. Tamarin filed suit in the District Court at Tel
Aviv in September, 1970 for a declaratory judgment and lost.
He appealed to the Supreme Court.

In its decision rendered on January 20, 1972 the Supreme
Court, by a vote of 3 to 0, ruled against Dr. Tamarin. Speak-
ing for the Court, Justice Shimon Agranat, then President of
the Supreme Court, stated that the desire of a small group
of Jews in Israel to separate and create an Israeli nation
separate from the Jewish nation was not a legitimate aspira-
tion. Splitting the people into Israeli and Jewish nations
would create a schism among the Jewish people and would
negate the very foundation on which the State of Israel was
formed.[114] "There is no Israeli nation separate from the Jewish people," Justice Agranat asserted. "The Jewish people is
composed not only of those residing in Israel but also of
Diaspora Jewry."[115] The Court continued to hold that Jewish
nationality and Israeli nationality are one and the same; that
is, nationality, as differentiated from citizenship, is synonymous with ethnicity insofar as Jews in Israel are concerned.[116]

Otto Preminger-Hope Price Matter, 1972

In 1959 Otto Preminger, the Jewish American movie director, married Hope Price, a non-Jewish American actress, in
Israel. Omitting the facts of Hope Price's non-Jewish ancestry, Otto Preminger was able to have an Orthodox rabbi
perform the marriage ceremony. The true facts in the story
were disclosed in 1971 when Meyer Weisgal's memoirs were
published.[117] Reaction among Israel's Orthodox rabbis was
severe, and doubts were expressed by the rabbinate in 1972
as to the validity of the marriage. However, by that time the
couple had returned to the United States. In any event, from
the Orthodox Jewish viewpoint the status as Jews of the two
children born to the couple is in doubt, and if the children
should ever apply to marry in Israel or to marry in an Orthodox Jewish ceremony anywhere they will have to prove that
their mother had converted to Judaism prior to their birth
or that they themselves had converted.[118]

Langer Case, 1972[119]

In 1924 in Poland Chava Ginsburg, a Jewess, became engaged to a Polish Catholic. At the insistence of Chava's
family the man converted to Judaism by an Orthodox rabbi
and assumed the name of Abraham Brokowsky. The following year the two were married in an Orthodox Jewish religious ceremony. Two sons were born to the couple. In 1933
the family emigrated from Poland and settled in Palestine,
where in 1941 the marriage fell apart. Three years later Chava
met and married Otto Langer, a Palestinian Jew. The Orthodox rabbi who performed the marriage ceremony in Palestine accepted Chava's claim that her first husband had been
a non-Jew and therefore she needed no religious divorce from

him. Two children, a son, Hanoch, and a daughter, Miriam, were born to the Langers.

As for Abraham Brokowsky, in 1951 he met another woman in Israel whom he wanted to marry. He applied to the Orthodox rabbinate for a divorce from Chava in order to remarry. Unaware of Chava's second marriage, the rabbinate granted the divorce. The following year Otto Langer died; and in 1955 Chava applied for a license to marry again. This time the rabbinate's record check disclosed the previous marriages of Chava to Brokowsky and Langer but no proof of a divorce from Brokowsky. Accordingly the Orthodox rabbinate, through the rabbinical court, registered the two Langer children as "mamzerim."

The word "mamzerim" is a Hebrew term, the plural of "mamzer." In Orthodox Jewish religious law a "mamzer" is a child born to a woman as a result of incest or to a married woman as a consequence of adultery. A "mamzer" is not synonymous with "bastard" or "illegitimate." A child born to an unmarried woman, other than by incest, is not a "mamzer." Moreover, a "mamzer" may not be legally married except to another "mamzer" or to a convert to Judaism. Such restrictions last until ten generations have passed.[120]

As no publicity is made of registrations of "mamzerim" the matter lay quiet for ten years, until Hanoch and Miriam Langer, both unaware of their registration as "mamzerim," applied to the Orthodox rabbinate for marriage licenses to marry Israeli Jews. They were then informed of their status and the marriage licenses were refused. They then applied to the rabbinical court for a procedure to follow which would change their registration from "mamzerim" to full-fledged, legitimate Jews. The rabbinical court rejected their application, as did the Supreme Rabbinical Court on appeal in 1970. The effect of such a ruling was to deny the Langer children the possibility of ever marrying a Jew who was not similarly a "mamzer" and to close off any door to legitimization.

Hanoch Langer, a sergeant-major in the Israeli army, took the matter personally to the Minister of Defense, Moshe Dayan; and the ensuing publicity prompted Gideon Hausner, a Member of the Knesset, to introduce a bill which would permit couples prevented from marrying by religious law to marry in civil ceremony. To forestall such a bill's passage Chief Rabbi Shlomo Goren of Israel's Ashkenazi community convened a special nine-member Supreme Rabbinical Court to consider the Langer case. Chief Rabbi Ovadia Yosef of Israel's Sephardic community, who had sat on the original Supreme Rabbinical Court which denied the Langer appeal in 1970, refused to serve on the court convened by Rabbi Goren.

On November 19, 1972 the special Supreme Rabbinical Court handed down its decision. It ruled that the two Langer children were not "mamzerim" and were full-fledged Jews free to marry any Jewish partners in Israel. The decision was based on four main grounds: (1) there was no evidence of a proper conversion to Judaism by Abraham Brokowsky in Poland; (2) even if the conversion had been proper, evidence showed that Abraham Brokowsky had never taken his conversion seriously and had reverted to Christian practices thereby nullifying the alleged conversion; (3) no adequate proof was available indicating a valid Orthodox Jewish marriage between Chava Ginsburg and Abraham Brokowsky; and (4) even if the alleged marriage was valid, Abraham Brokowsky's filing of an application for a divorce from Chava automatically nullified the original marriage. Accordingly, Chava's marriage to Langer was valid, and the two children born of the latter union were legitimate. The registration of Hanoch and Miriam Langer was changed, and their marriages to Jewish partners were performed in an Orthodox Jewish ceremony and registered as valid.[121]

The decision was accepted by a majority of Israelis, including many of the moderate elements of Orthodox Jewry.

However, a significant number of Orthodox Jews, particularly the ultra-Orthodox, were bitterly incensed. One day after the ruling, four ultra-Orthodox students attacked Rabbi Goren as he walked in a funeral procession;[122] and a letter bomb sent to Rabbi Goren's home was believed by the police to have been mailed by ultra-Orthodox opponents.[123] The Sephardic Chief Rabbi, Ovadia Yosef, maintaining that he was duped into signing the wedding certificates of the Langer children, tore up his copies in public display.[124]

When apprised of the decision, Abraham Brokowsky appealed to the Supreme Court of Israel to have Rabbi Goren's ruling and the record of his court made public. In addition, Brokowsky complained that the Goren tribunal denied him his rights to have appeared and presented his side and that the decision was based on an erroneous fact that he was not a practicing Jew. The Supreme Court directed Rabbi Goren to explain within thirty days why he had not published the records in the *Langer* case and also to refrain from making any public statement alleging that Abraham Brokowsky was not a Jew and to prove to the Supreme Court that he was not a practicing Jew. After explaining to the Supreme Court how his court reached its decision and then publishing the full record of the *Langer* case, the Supreme Court on April 3, 1973 held that Rabbi Goren had complied with its orders and was satisfied that the Goren tribunal's ruling was based on substantial testimony by honorable witnesses indicating Abraham Brokowsky had not observed Jewish practices and had reverted to Christianity.[125] As for Brokowsky's desire to present his side personally to Goren's court, Rabbi Goren explained to the Supreme Court that Brokowsky had presented his side in complete detail to the first rabbinical court convened to hear the problem in 1966 and that according to Orthodox religious law an individual may appear before a rabbinical court only once in a given case.[126]

In what appeared to have been a gesture of conciliation to

the ultra-Orthodox opposition, Rabbi Goren, shortly after his decision in the *Langer* case, announced that he would press the Knesset to amend Israel's Law of Return so that conversions to Judaism would have to be "according to "halachah" (traditional Orthodox religious law), a provision which would mean that all conversions to Judaism performed by rabbis of other than the Orthodox denomination would not be recognized in Israel. This issue is discussed later in detail. One immediate effect of the Goren ruling was that it brought about a postponement of Gideon Hausner's bill in the Knesset, thereby saving the Coalition Government from another serious political crisis.

Actually the *Langer* case was not a matter of "Who Is A Jew?" so much as it was a question of "Who Is A Non-Jewish Jew?" The majority of Israeli Jews are opposed to the creation of a special class of Jews who are deemed by ultra-Orthodox standards to be outcasts, simultaneously Jews and yet not Jews. This was acknowledged especially by Orthodox Rabbi Zvi Yehuda Kook, son of Israel's revered late Orthodox Chief Rabbi Abraham Isaac Kook and head of the Kook Yeshiva in Jerusalem, who praised Rabbi Goren's decision.[127] While the *Langer* case is now history, its repercussions on Jewry world-wide were great and profound. In Israel, however, each dilemma, issue and crisis has little time to run full course, for they are soon replaced by new problems.

Yeshayahu Shik Case, 1973[128]

Yeshayahu Shik entered Israel at the age of eleven and was registered by his mother as a Jew in both nationality ("le'um") and religion. At sixteen he applied for his own identity card; and on the application form he refused to fill in the declarations of nationality and religion stating that he wished to be considered a cosmopolitan. His primary argument was that his mother had registered him without his knowledge or consent when he was a child. In requesting the changes Shik emphasized that he was not cutting himself away from the Jewish community. The Ministry of the Interior agreed to delete only the entry regarding religion but refused with respect to nationality. Shik then petitioned the District Court for a public document (certificate) under Sec. 19C of the Population Registry Law of 1965 as amended in 1967 and 1970 to direct the change in registration be made.[129] The District Court denied the application. Shik appealed to the Supreme Court.

On April 29, 1973 the Supreme Court unanimously ruled in Shik's favor. The registration by his mother when he was eleven could not hold forever and he had the right to change it. Following the Court's decision in the *I. Ben Monashe* case of 1970 Justice Zvi Berinson declared that since any person may, at the original registration, request that the spaces for nationality and religion be left blank then certainly the right of omission or deletion should be granted to a person whose first registration was effected without his or her consent. Shik's attorney was I. Ben Menashe who won his own case before the Supreme Court three years earlier. Actually Ben Menashe had requested that his children be registered without any entry as to nationality ("le'um"); but the Court ruled that omissions of entries are legal, implying that the entry as to religion likewise may be omitted. The *Shik* case took that ruling one step further and positively authorized the omission or deletion of the entry as to religion, too. The Court's reasoning was logical in also implying that since it was permissible for a child whose mother had registered him or her as without religion to change later that registration to Jewish as his mother is or was a Jew, why then should the person be deprived of the right to accomplish the reverse?

A long road had been covered by the *Shik* decision. It had

now become possible for an Israeli to be registered as without nationality ("le'um") and without religion. However, with regard to changes from one nationality ("le'um") or religion to another, the Supreme Court, in order to avoid capricious changes in registrations, stressed the necessity of proving that the requested changes were genuine and seriously considered.[130]

Case of the American Black Israelites, 1969–1973[131]

In December, 1969 a group of thirty-nine American Blacks from Chicago who called themselves "Hebrew Israelites" left a settlement in Liberia after becoming dissatisfied and emigrated to Israel contending they were Hebrews and entitled to automatic citizenship authorized under the Law of Return. They were allowed to remain temporarily as tourists in Israel pending decision whether to admit them as Jews. The immigration authorities announced publicly that the thirty-nine were admitted "as Americans with American passports, not as new immigrants."[132]

This was not the usual matter which vexed Israel's religious circles. Here the Orthodox rabbinate itself was divided. The thirty-nine Blacks insisted they were descendants of the biblical patriarchs Abraham, Isaac and Jacob and of the Twelve Tribes of ancient Israel and were Hebrews who observed the practices of the Old Testament and consequently must be considered Hebrews. The Israeli secular authorities granted the group temporary residency and assisted them in settling in a new desert town, Dimona. However, the religious authorities insisted that the group members formally convert to Orthodox Judaism. This the Blacks refused, maintaining they already were Hebrews. As later groups of Black

Israelites arrived, the secular authorities began to take a harder line, particularly since the Blacks became more emphatic in insisting they were not Jews but were Hebrew Israelites and were questioning the right of European and Middle Eastern Jews to live in Israel. "We want them to remain," stated Black Israelite leader Ben-Ami Carter, "if they recognize us as the children of the God of Israel."[133]

The issue unresolved, in August, 1971 the Black Israelites congregated in front of the Zion Gate of the Old City of Jerusalem and at a news conference protested that both the religious and secular authorities were discriminating against them by failing to provide jobs and decent housing and by practicing "Jim Crow policies."[134] Members of the group, by now numbering at least 300, most of whom emigrated directly from the United States, were denied resident status and were given tourist status and therefore were unable to qualify for housing, medical care, job assistance, or educational benefits and were barred from claiming citizenship. Most of the Black Israelites lived in desert settlements in the Negev, particularly in Dimona, Arad and Mitzpeh Rimon.

On October 7, 1971 twenty-one additional American Black Israelites who arrived in Israel the previous day were denied immigrant or tourist status and were deported. The leader of this group, Kolayah, a 27-year old community worker from Chicago, insisted that the Israeli Jews were essentially white Europeans "who have adopted our culture" whereas "Moses was black and Jesus Christ was black." As for the other 200 or more Black Israelites still in Israel on visitors' visas, the Ministry of the Interior announced it would decide their status as their visas expired.[135] On December 19, 1971 the Ministry ordered the deportation of eight Black Israelites who had arrived in October on one-month tourist visas and who had not renewed their visas contending they were in their homeland and were not obliged to obtain tourist visas to stay.[136] The eight petitioned the Supreme Court, and on

January 23, 1972 the Court issued an order calling on the Minister of the Interior to show cause why the deportation order should not be cancelled.[137] Deciding it would further study the matter the Ministry held off the deportations.

The following September, however, the Government announced that it was planning to deport all the American Black Israelites.[138] In October a group of the Black Israelites petitioned the American Embassy in Israel to accept their renunciation of American citizenship; and as stateless persons they would then appeal to Israeli and world opinion to force the Government of Israel to grant them the right to remain in Israel.[139] In addition, suit was filed by the Black Israelites in the Israeli courts to rescind all expulsion orders and to direct the Minister of the Interior to grant citizenship to them as Jews under the Law of Return. In October, 1973 the Supreme Court ruled that the Black Israelites were not Jews within the meaning of the Law of Return. As a result of this decision, those Black Israelites comprising a criminal element were deported, while the others have remained without any final resolution as yet of their status as residents.[140]

Proposed Amendments to the Law of Return, 1972-1974

The *Zeidman* case sharply pointed up a gap in Orthodox rabbinical ability to control the defining of who is a Jew with regard to the Law of Return. If conversions to Judaism within Israel were required to conform solely to Orthodox rabbinical procedures, then it would be possible for a person converted to Judaism outside of Israel by other than Orthodox religious authorities to be considered a Jew outside of Israel and then to be admitted into Israel as a Jew under the Law of Return; whereas a person converted to Judaism within Israel by other than Orthodox religious procedures would not be registered as a Jew. This possibility disturbed the Israeli Orthodox rabbinate, and in June, 1972 it introduced, through two of its Knesset Members, Rabbi Shlomo Lorincz and Rabbi Kalman Kahana, two bills to amend the Law of Return by defining converts to Judaism as persons whose conversions were accomplished in accordance with Orthodox rabbinical procedures only.[141]

Virtually identical, Lorincz's and Kahana's bills contained two sections. One dealt with conversions; and the other would deny immigrants any of the material rights and privileges ordinarily accorded to Jewish immigrants, if they are non-Jewish parties to or the offspring of mixed marriages, to the third generation, even though the Jewish member of the family may no longer be alive or may not desire to immigrate to Israel. These privileges were provided by the 1970 Amendment to the Law of Return. The two bills were supported by uncompromising Orthodox elements inside and outside of Israel who severely criticized those Orthodox Cabinet Ministers and Knesset Members who agreed to the 1970 Amendment. To move the bills quickly through the Knesset Rabbi Lorincz laid down an eight-day ultimatum to the Cabinet to indicate how it would vote on them. If it failed to take a stand, or if it opposed the bills but would not permit the Orthodox Cabinet Ministers to abstain, then the latter would resign from the Government causing the Government to fall and precipitating a new general election. The impending crisis occurred just as another Cabinet crisis abated, over a Knesset bill authorizing civil marriages between couples ineligible to be wed by Israel's rabbinate. The latter crisis dissipated when Chief Rabbi Shlomo Goren's special court handed down its ruling in the *Langer* case, as a result of which the Knesset postponed voting on the civil marriage bill introduced by Gideon Hausner.

On July 12, 1972 the Lorincz and Kahana bills were taken up by the Knesset and were defeated by a vote of 57 to 19, with 11 abstentions. The National Religious Party's Ministers in the Cabinet, initially intent on supporting the bills, reversed themselves and abstained after Premier Meir warned them that an affirmative vote would violate Cabinet discipline and endanger the Coalition's existence but that abstention would be allowed.[142] During the debate on the bills in the Knesset Premier Meir castigated those of the Orthodox rabbinate who ignored the political and social effects of such proposed legislation. "It is impossible," she angrily remarked, "to continue under the strictures of ancient customs. Our rabbis must find a way to ease the nation's burdens."[143] "I am saying this with full responsibility," the Prime Minister further warned, "I know very many irreligious people who do not want to see a split—but it will happen unless the majority of the public is relieved of crushing rules with which it cannot live." The debate was bitter. "Why had there not been any cases of mamzerim in the shtetl (European ghetto village) of old?," Premier Meir asked. A rabbinical Member of the Knesset replied, "Because people were moral." Retorted the Prime Minister: "No, that was not the reason. The reason was that the rabbis were greater scholars and at the same time far more compassionate human beings than the rabbis of today."[144]

While the abstention votes of the National Religious Party could not have prevented defeat of the Lorincz and Kahana bills had they been opposition votes, the criticism from many Orthodox rabbinical groups within and outside of Israel was vehement, if not abusive. Actually, in return for the abstention, the Cabinet agreed to postpone the Hausner civil marriage bill indefinitely when it would come before the Knesset after the summer recess.[145] Many Orthodox supporters of the Lorincz and Kahana bills scoffed at this agreement and insisted that the Hausner bill would be defeated on its own by the opposition of many Mapai Party Members in addition to the Orthodox Jewish, Moslem and Christian Members who opposed civil marriage.

By January, 1974 Premier Meir's Mapai Party needed more than ever the votes of the National Religious Party to give the Government a secure majority in the Knesset. However, the National Religious Party demanded, as the price for its support, that the Law of Return be amended to recognize only Orthodox religious conversions to Judaism. This created a furor in Jewish Conservative and Reform circles abroad whose support Israel vitally needed, particularly at that time. Some Conservative rabbis suggested that an

amended Law of Return which simply states that all conversions must be performed in accordance with "halachic principle," rather than "halachah" would be accepted by Conservative Jewry.[146] This would enable the non-Orthodox
rabbis to perform conversions as long as they followed the
principles of "halachah." No favorable response was elicited
from Israel's Orthodox rabbis. However, Great Britain's Orthodox Chief Rabbi, Dr. Immanuel Jakobovits, went even
further by advocating a separation of religion and politics
and by favoring some form of civil marriage in hardship
cases in Israel. He deplored Israel's religious political parties
because they were not responsible to communities of people
as ordinary political parties are. With regard to "Who Is a
Jew?" he urged that secular law and the secular authorities
should be concerned with "Who Is An Israeli?" and that
religious law and the religious authorities should be concerned with "Who Is A Jew?"[147] Unfortunately, the problem
is not that simple, and Rabbi Jakobovits' suggestion does not
really solve it.

In February, 1974 the Chief Rabbinical Council ordered
the National Religious Party not to enter any new coalition
government which would not pledge to amend the Law of
Return so as to invalidate non-Orthodox conversions to Judaism. This prevented compromise and the formation of a
government by Golda Meir. The struggle became so grim
that an attorney, acting as an individual citizen in the public
interest, petitioned the Supreme Court to order the rabbinical bodies to cease interfering with the secular political process of forming a government. On March 6, 1974 the Supreme
Court issued an order nisi directing the Chief Rabbinical
Council to show cause within two weeks why it should not
revoke its instruction to the National Religious Party not to
join the coalition government, and then issued a temporary
injunction barring the rabbinical authorities from enforcing
their ban pending the Supreme Court's final decision.[148] The
case was fixed for hearing on April 18. In the meantime

Premier Meir pleaded with the National Religious Party to join the coalition for reason of national unity in the face of danger from the surrounding Arab nations. The National Religious Party, with ten seats in the Knesset at the time, agreed to join the coalition government after Premier Meir and the proposed cabinet accepted the principle that conversions to Judaism should be according to Orthodox religious law and, also, that a cabinet committee headed by the Prime Minister would attempt to reach a settlement within a year of the issue of conversions. The agreement provided, further, that the Minister of the Interior would issue a statement that to the best of his knowledge no non-Jew had been registered as a Jew in the last four years.[149]

The new Government was presented to the Knesset on March 10, 1974, and the matter before the Supreme Court lost all practical import and the petitioner therefore canceled his petition. However, on March 21, the Minister of the Interior, a member of the National Religious Party, announced that he would refuse to register immigrant converts to Judaism unless they had been converted by Orthodox rabbis and that this policy would be followed until the ministerial committee completed its attempt to solve the problem. Many ultra-Orthodox elements in Israel and abroad were opposed to waiting out the year and urged the National Religious Party to withdraw from the Government unless it could obtain assurances that legislation would be introduced and supported which would amend the Law of Return immediately. In the midst of this mounting dissention there was issued the report of the special commission investigating the military shortcomings of Israel at the beginning of the Yom Kippur War in October, 1973. Those issues led to Premier Golda Meir's resignation and retirement from political life on April 10, 1974; and with the fall of the Government, the ministerial committee appointed to examine the conversion problem was dissolved.

A new Government, headed by Prime Minister Yitzhak

Rabin and excluding the National Religious Party, was approved by the Knesset on June 3, 1974. The National Party refused to enter the Government unless the Law of Return would be amended to prohibit recognition of conversions performed by other than Orthodox rabbis in accordance with Orthodox religious law ("halachah"). Having joined with other political parties which opposed the National Religious Party to form his Government, Premier Rabin did not press for the National Religious Party to join the Coalition. His Coalition partners have been against any further concession to the National Religious Party for fear of alienating many non-Orthodox Jews abroad who have been the main supporters of Israel.[150]

Recognizing that it could better achieve its goals within the Government than outside, the National Religious Party voted in September, 1974 to convey to Premier Rabin its willingness to join the Coalition on condition that the registration of immigrants converted to Judaism abroad be suspended for one year, and that a ministerial committee be established to study the conversion issue and find an acceptable solution within the one year period. However, the Independent Liberal Party and the Citizens Rights Party, together commanding seven seats in the Knesset, voted on September 13, 1974 to withdraw from the Coalition if Premier Rabin did not reject the compromise proposal of the National Religious Party. On the following October 17 Prime Minister Rabin, in the interest of national unity, invited the National Religious Party to join the Coalition without any pre-conditions but with the promise that the conversion issue would be taken up by a special ministerial committee to be created when the National Religious Party enters the Government and that a settlement agreeable to all parties in the Coalition would be sought.

The Independent Liberal Party indicated it would go along with Premier Rabin's offer but would oppose in the ministerial committee any recommendation for a freeze on immigration registrations involving conversions abroad; and the Citizens Rights Party hinted it might follow the approach of the Independent Liberal Party. On October 24 the National Religious Party voted to join the Government. Premier Rabin had agreed to give four ministerial portfolios to the National Religious Party if it joined the Coalition and delivered all its ten votes in the Knesset in support of the Government. However, three Knesset Members of the National Religious Party refused to support the Government; and consequently Premier Rabin gave the National Religious Party only three Cabinet portfolios including those of Minister of Religious Affairs and Minister of the Interior. On the other hand, Mrs. Shulamit Aloni, head of the Citizens Rights Party, disapproved of the acceptance of the National Religious Party in the Government and resigned from the Coalition pulling out three Knesset votes for Premier Rabin's Government. These moves gave Rabin a net gain of four parliamentary seats. On October 31, 1974 the Knesset approved the inclusion of the National Religious Party in the Government.[151]

As of the summer of 1975, the time of this writing, the issue of conversions to Judaism abroad and the entire question of "Who Is A Jew? have not provoked any further action by the Knesset, Government, or political parties, primarily because of the grave problems of foreign affairs and national survival.

Conclusion: Is There a Solution?

Seventeen years have passed since the "Who Is A Jew?" question first arose in Israel as a crisis provoking political and legal dilemma. From the beginning the question involved the Cabinet, Knesset, rabbinical and secular authorities, and an aroused, highly politicized Jewish public. The ensuing cases and incidents all have had a common denominator—the relationship of religion and state; but the immediate issues over which the conflicts have been fought have kept shifting, including such issues as immigration and citizenship, conversions from Judaism to Christianity, religious and civil marriage and divorce, ethnic and racial origins, marriages prohibited by rabbinical law, atheism, and conversions to Judaism by other than Orthodox rabbis. "Who Is A Jew?" has not been the only arena in which conflicts have arisen over the role of religion in Israeli society. Bitter controversies have erupted over other matters, such as a secular constitution for the nation, education, autopsies, military service for women, operation of vehicles on the Sabbath, males and females bathing in the same swimming pools at the same time, abattoirs, and the production, importation and serving of non-kosher foods.

In all these conflicts involving the relationship of religion and state the power of the Orthodox religious authorities was apparent. While to adherents of Orthodoxy such power is accepted and approved, it has caused long simmering resentment among non-Orthodox Jews in Israel and abroad, particularly among those who see in Orthodox concepts and practices national backwardness and also medieval attitudes toward women and marriage. So bitter has this resentment been that Golda Meir, while Prime Minister, angrily criticized the Israeli Orthodox rabbinate on April 3, 1971 during a special Cabinet meeting on the issue of "Who Is A Jew?": "If God has to be compassionate, then rabbis also have to be compassionate!"[152] What prompted the outburst was that the Israeli Orthodox rabbinate questioned the procedure being employed in Vienna to convert quickly the non-Jewish spouses of Jews emigrating from the Soviet Union to Israel. In order to encourage the Russian Jews to immigrate to Israel, the Israeli Government was willing to overlook the extent of their Judaism and therefore arranged for hasty conversions to enable them to enter Israel as Jews under the Law of Return.

If compassion is what is required of the Orthodox rabbinate in Israel as called for by Golda Meir, rationality is what is more desired by non-Orthodox Jewry in Israel and abroad, particularly in cases in which the offspring of non-Jewish mothers and Jewish fathers are being raised as Jews and participate in Jewish social and cultural life. Are such persons less Jewish than atheists born to Jewish mothers but who do not participate in and support Jewish causes? Are such persons less Jewish than the Palestinian Arab terrorist who is deemed a Jew because he was born to a Jewish mother?

Since the Supreme Court of Israel has decided it permissible to omit registration entries under nationality ("le'um") and religion in the Population Register and on individual identity cards, it may well ultimately be that rationality will demand the cessation of registering nationality and perhaps even religion for secular purposes. This could go a long way to solving the dilemma. In the meantime, however, the dilemma exists; and the inflexibility of the Orthodox rabbinate in Israel is considered a virtue by those who feel that there is but one banner of Judaism and it is being carried only by Orthodox Jews marching behind a drummer called "halachah" (traditional Orthodox religious law) and on a road labeled "survival." The underlying justifications presented for this inflexibility are the fears of intermarriage, assimilation and loss of Jews to Christianity, and secular inroads of agnosticism and atheism. Yet, the history of Judaism reveals the fundamental principle of humanism with its legal corollary that every grievance should have a remedy in the lifetime of an aggrieved. To have cleaved the Langer children from full-fledged Judaism and offered no remedy was a violation of the humanistic principle of Judaism. While Chief Rabbi Shlomo Goren provided the remedy in the *Langer* case, the hopes he raised for consistent humanism were short-lived.

If the question of "Who Is A Jew?" were confined to registration of religion and would have no secular application it would have caused no great conflicts or problems; but with the addition of the registration requirement of nationality, meaning ethnic affiliation, and by applying both religion and nationality to secular laws—and with the Orthodox rabbinical authorities operating through political parties and governmental agencies and rejecting compromise and recognition of any Conservative and Reform rabbinical authority —the question of "Who Is A Jew?" became an impossible dilemma. In assessing the dilemma's current status, one will note first that all attempts in Israel to authorize civil marriage and divorce and the performance of valid marriages and conversions by Conservative and Reform rabbis thus far have failed, and second that the issue on which the dilemma focuses at the present time is conversions to Judaism abroad by other than Orthodox procedures. This matter of conversions has become an acrimonious and divisive issue in Israel with sharp repercussions in Jewish communities throughout the world. When one examines the procedures for conversion among the three major Jewish denominations—Orthodox, Conservative and Reform—one does not find such great differences that reasonably should result in the bitter conflicts that have arisen. However, the issue essentially is not how one is converted to Judaism but by whom. Authority and power, not procedure, constitute the key to understanding the problem.

Nevertheless, it is appropriate to know what the principles and procedures are with regard to becoming a Jew by conversion. If the conversion is by the Orthodox denomination, they are: (1) a statement of intention to an Orthodox rabbi; (2) pursuit of an intensive, prolonged course of instruction with an Orthodox rabbi and passing of a test on the Bible, prayer book, customs and rituals, holiday observances, and Jewish history; (3) immersion in the traditional ritual bath ("tehvilah") in a pool of running water coming directly from a natural spring or a river ("mikveh"); and (4) circumcision for male applicants. After these steps have been taken, the applicant appears before an Orthodox rabbi and, in the presence of two other Orthodox rabbis or learned Orthodox Jewish laymen, declares that he or she understands and accepts the duties and obligations of Jewish religious law and tradition, rejects those tenets of his or her former faith which differ from those of Judaism, has been baptized in the traditional ritual bath, and, if male, has been circumcised. Both male and female applicants are required to pronounce the same blessing on emerging from the ritual bath: "Blessed art thou, Lord our God, King of the universe who hast sanctified

us with thy commandments, and commanded us about immersion."

On the following Sabbath the male convert is called to the
reading of the Torah in the synagogue and recites this special
blessing: "May He Who blessed our ancestor, Abraham, the
first convert, and said to him, 'Go thou before Me and be
righteous,' bless and give courage to this convert who enters
the fold." As a male convert he is then given the Hebrew
name "Abraham" for use in religious ceremonies and ritual
acts.[153] With these steps taken, the applicant must be accepted into the Jewish community and considered a full-
fledged Jew, with one exception if he or she is single—marriage to another convert to Judaism is forbidden. However,
a non-Jewish married couple may be converted simultaneously and remain married to each other. In nearly all other
respects, the convert must be treated as if he or she were a
Jew by birth. A special difference is made between single
male and female converts in that the male may marry the
daughter of a "Cohen," but the female may not marry a
"Cohen." If a female applicant is pregnant she must be converted prior to the birth of the child in order for the child
to be deemed a Jew automatically by birth; otherwise the
child will later have to undergo conversion. Converts to
Orthodox Judaism are required also to oberve the Sabbath
dietary laws ("kashruth") and the laws of purity ("Tohoroth"); and women, in addition, must observe the laws of
female ritual cleanliness ("Niddah"). Mixed praying, swimming and dancing are prohibited.

The procedure of Conservative Judaism is similar to that
of the Orthodox with Conservative rabbis guiding the conversion process. However, ritual immersion may be conducted on a mass, rather than an individual, basis with males
and females together and in an ordinary swimming pool
instead of a "mikveh." Also, mixed praying and dancing are
permissible. It is with regard to Reform Judaism that the

conversion procedure differs somewhat, though not greatly. The convert must: (1) announce his or her intention to a Reform rabbi; (2) pursue a six-month course of instruction with testing under guidance of a Reform rabbi; (3) declare that he or she has renounced the former faith, and pledge loyalty to Judaism; and (4) promise to cast his or her lot with the people of Israel in all circumstances and conditions, to raise all offspring in the Jewish faith, and to have himself, if male, and all male children, undergo circumcision. With this formal pledge made to a Reform rabbi, the applicant repeats in Hebrew and native language the prayer: "Hear O Israel, the Lord our God, the Lord is One." The convert is then considered a full-fledged Jew. No ritual immersion is required. Unlike his or her Orthodox counterpart, the Reform convert is not restricted from marrying another convert; and observance of the Sabbath, dietary laws, ritual immersion, redemption of the firstborn son, head covering by the male, and mixed praying, dancing and swimming is optional. Affiliation with a temple and engagement in Jewish community activities are encouraged.

As the *Brother Daniel* case emphasized, a person ceases to be a Jew when he adopts another religion. Yet, he can become a Jew again by renouncing the other religion and undergoing an abbreviated conversion procedure required by each of three major denominations of Judaism, except that the Orthodox practice requires the person to undergo ritual immersion under the direction of three Orthodox guides, one of whom must be a rabbi.[154] All three denominations require that an applicant for conversion, whether it is an original conversion or a return to Judaism, must accept Judaism out of inner conviction and without ulterior motives. The conversion must not be motivated by fear of punishment[155] or in order to marry.[156]

As the Orthodox rabbinate in Israel does not recognize a conversion to Judaism performed abroad by Conservative or

Reform rabbis, and does not permit Conservative or Reform rabbis to perform marriages, divorces and conversions in Israel, the question of "Who Is A Jew?" takes on a quality of divisiveness, bitter conflict, and long-term provocation. A compromise proposal was recently made by a number of Jewish thinkers which called on the three major denominations to form joint local committees or courts to set common, accepted standards for conversions and to supervise their implementation.[157]

The Orthodox rabbinate does not and probably will not agree to such a proposal. Under Israel's present multi-political party system with coalition cabinets the practical rule, the Orthodox rabbinate, operating through the National Religious Party and commanding a sizable bloc of seats in the Knesset and a number of ministerial portfolios in the Cabinet, has taken and probably will continue to take advantage of its political power to prevent or postpone the adoption of any proposal for significant change in the relationship of religion and state generally and for recognition of Conservative and Reform conversions to Judaism in particular. Yet, there are prominent Orthodox thinkers who have been critical of Israel's Orthodox rabbinate and religious parties. For example, Rabbi Joseph B. Soloveitchik, Dean of Yeshiva University's Rabbinical Seminary in New York City and a leader of Orthodox Jewry in the United States, has long requested Israel's rabbinate to withdraw from politics and that the National Religious Party and all other religious parties be disbanded. This recommendation has been strongly supported by Professor Efrayim E. Urbach of the Hebrew University at Jerusalem, who is a leading Orthodox scholar and member of the National Religious Party.[158]

It is estimated that 85% of the Jewish population of Israel are more secular minded than religious oriented and do not adhere to or support the Orthodox denomination; yet they submit to and accept the Orthodox religious authority and the Orthodox system of rabbinical laws governing many of the most important personal aspects of their lives. It may be that the Israeli Jews, beset with a myriad of political, economic and social problems feel that the problem of the relationship of religion and state will be considered later after the more pressing problems of national security and international relations are resolved.

Being realistic and pragmatic in its foreign policies, Israel is no different in its domestic policies. The majority of Israelis know that the last codification of the Orthodox system of religious laws occurred over 400 years ago and that the system was geared to life and survival as Jews in exile. They know, too, that while there have been piecemeal reinterpretations of the system no over-all recodification has since taken place to reflect changing times, particularly the existence of the modern State of Israel. That this someday will occur most Israelis do feel, although it is deemed a long-range, slow and gradual affair. Nevertheless, it seems that the early, active anti-religious sentiment of the Israeli Jewish settlers is giving way to a relatively passive, non-religious attitude with an increasing tolerance of the religious Jews. The converse, on the other hand, does not appear to be true. Accordingly, the secular minded majority, fearful of splitting the country in the present period of national peril and acknowledging the feelings of Christians and Moslems the world over for the Holy Land, have not pressed for strict separation of religion and state or for banning religious political parties. However, there is a strong desire for certain reforms in religious laws to conform with modern concepts of democracy, particularly regarding women's rights and personal status. In any event, the vast majority of Israelis know there is no danger that their nation might be transformed into a theocratic state. The secular Supreme Court, if not the Knesset, stands powerfully in the way of such a development. The Court has long held that it is competent to review the judgments of the religious courts and to check abuses of religious powers.[159]

The "Who Is A Jew?" question is not matched by "Who Is An Arab?" though Arabs proclaim an "Arab nation" to which belong all Arabs, whether Moslem or Christian in religion and regardless of which country they hold citizenship in. When Israeli Arabs are registered in the national Population Register they are recorded as Arab in nationality ("le'um") and generally as Moslem, Greek Catholic or Greek Orthodox in religion. Similarly, Jews assert a "Jewish nation"; but, unlike the Arabs, the Jews have one religion. However, the Orthodox rabbinical authorities in Israel do not deem Jews of the Conservative or Reform denominations to be full-fledged members of the "Jewish nation." This view, coupled with the denial to the Conservative and Reform rabbinates of the right in Israel to perform marriages, divorces and conversions, ignores the realities of modern Judaism and consequently tends to evoke bitterness and division among world Jewry, particularly among Jews in the United States. Interestingly, in the Soviet Union, which asserts the existence of "a Jewish nation," the identity card bearing the entry "Jew" indicates the person's Jewish nationality, not his religion. Accordingly, a gentile who converts to Judaism in the Soviet Union would not have his identity card changed to read "Jew."

When one realizes that the "Arab nation" numbers over 100 million adherents while the "Jewish nation" has a worldwide membership of only about 14 1/2 million after having lost 6 million to Nazi Germany's "final solution" and today barely reproducing its own numbers, it requires no great intellect to point out that each member of the "Jewish nation" should be preciously and equally prized. In a related respect, the point must be made that no one Jewish group should proclaim that it represents all or the best of Jewry and that its mission is to lead, save or speak for world Jewry. It must be understood that there are no one ethnic mold, no single language, and no uniform set of religious customs acknowledged by all Jews throughout the world. In the Far East there are Chinese and Japanese Jews who are of the Yellow Race. In Southern Europe there are swarthy Italian and Greek Jews. In India, Ethiopia and New York City there are Black Jews; and in North Africa there are Jews who are brown in skin pigmentation. Unfortunately, the fact of being a Jew with black or brown skin color in Israel has resulted in discrimination by white Orthodox and non-Orthodox fellow Jews.

While repercussions of the "Who Is A Jew?" question have resounded in countries outside of Israel, it is essentially the State of Israel which directly faces the dilemma in its full political and legal dimensions, and it is Israel which will have to make the decisions. In view of the grave danger to Israel's national survival from the surrounding Arab nations and their supporters, the question of "Who Is A Jew?" has temporarily receded in priority. That it will again arise appears inevitable. That it will be resolved in the near future, however, is unlikely. Such proposals as excluding Orthodox religious law ("halachah") from secular legislation, acknowledging that a Jew is anyone who states he or she is a Jew, excluding or withdrawing of religious parties from politics, permitting civil marriages even in the limited area of religiously banned unions, rescinding the Law of Return, or eliminating registration entries as to nationality and perhaps also religion from the Population Register and individual identity cards are remote possibilities. On the other hand, such suggestions as curtailing the registration of all converts except those from the Soviet Union or moratoriums on registering all immigrant converts are temporary, stalling measures affecting only one aspect of the complex problem. The suggestion that the word "Hebrew" replace "Jew" to designate nationality (ethnic affiliation) and be employed in a strictly secular sense may have some merit in eliminating the use of the same word for both nationality and religion, but it will not solve the basic legal dilemma.[160] What is sorely needed now, as a first step, is the acceptance by the three major Jewish religious denominations—Conservative, Orthodox and Reform—of each other's members as full-fledged Jews, which implies mutual recognition of marriages, divorces and conversions performed by the respective rabbis according to agreeable minimum standards.[161] If even this is unattainable then the dilemma of "Who Is A Jew?" is indeed to be marked an eternal impossibility.[162]

Appendices

No. 48

LAW OF RETURN, 5710—1950*

Right of aliya1).

1. Every Jew has the right to come to this country as an *oleh*1).

Oleh's visa.

2. (a) *Aliyah* shall be by *oleh's* visa.

(b) An *oleh's* visa shall be granted to every Jew who has expressed his desire to settle in Israel, unless the Minister of Immigration is satisfied that the applicant —

(1) is engaged in an activity directed against the Jewish people; or

(2) is likely to endanger public health or the security of the State.

'Oleh's certificate.

3. (a) A Jew who has come to Israel and subsequent to his arrival has expressed his desire to settle in Israel may, while still in Israel, receive an *oleh's* certificate.

(b) The restrictions specified in section 2(b) shall apply also to the grant of an *oleh's* certificate, but a person shall not be regarded as endangering public health on account of an illness contracted after his arrival in Israel.

Residents and persons born in this country.

4. Every Jew who has immigrated into this country before the coming into force of this Law, and every Jew who was born in this country, whether before or after the coming into force of this Law, shall be deemed to be a person who has come to this country as an *'oleh* under this Law.

Implementation and regulations.

5. The Minister of Immigration is charged with the implementation of this Law and may make regulations as to any matter relating to such implementation and also as to the grant of *oleh's* visas and *oleh's* certificates to minors up to the age of 18 years.

DAVID BEN-GURION   MOSHE SHAPIRA
Prime Minister   *Minister of Immigration*

YOSEF SPRINZAK
Acting President of the State
Chairman of the Knesset

---

* Passed by the Knesset on the 20th Tammuz, 5710 (5th July, 1950) and published in *Sefer Ha-Chukkim* No. 51 of the 21st Tammuz, 5710 (5th July, 1950), p. 159; the Bill and an Explanatory Note were published in *Hatza'ot Chok* No. 48 of the 12th Tammuz, 5710 (27th June, 1950), p. 189.

1) Translator's Note: *aliya* means immigration of Jews, and *oleh* (plural: *olim*) means a Jew immigrating, into Israel.

Reproduced from the Laws of the State of Israel, *Vol. 4 (5710–1949/50), p. 114.*

No. 55

LAW OF RETURN (AMENDMENT) 5714—1954*

Amendment of section 2 (b).

1. In section 2 (b) of the Law of Return, 5710—1950[1]) —

(1) the full stop at the end of paragraph (2) shall be replaced by a semi-colon, and the word "or" shall be inserted thereafter ;

(2) the following paragraph shall be inserted after paragraph (2):
"(3) is a person with a criminal past, likely to endanger public welfare.".

Amendment of sections 2 and 5.

2. In sections 2 and 5 of the Law, the words "the Minister of Immigration" shall be replaced by the words "the Minister of the Interior".

MOSHE SHARETT　　　　YOSEF SERLIN
Prime Minister　　　　*Minister of Health*
Acting Minister of the Interior

YITZCHAK BEN-ZVI
President of the State

---

* Passed by the Knesset on the 24th Av, 5714 (23rd August, 1954) and published in *Sefer Ha-Chukkim* No. 163 of the 3rd Elul, 5714 (1st September, 1954) p. 174; the Bill and an Explanatory Note were published in *Hatza'ot Chok* No. 192 of 5714, p. 88.

1) *Sefer Ha-Chukkim* No. 51 of 5710, p. 159; *LSI* vol. IV, p. 114.

(No. 20)

LAW OF RETURN (AMENDMENT NO. 2), 5730—1970 *

Addition of
sections 4A
and 4B.

1.　In the Law of Return, 5710—1950 [1]), the following sections shall be inserted after section 4 :

"Rights of
members of
family.

4A. (a) The rights of a Jew under this Law and the rights of an *oleh* under the Nationality Law, 5712—1952 [2]), as well as the rights of an *oleh* under any other enactment, are also vested in a child and a grandchild of a Jew, the spouse of a Jew, the spouse of a child of a Jew and the spouse of a grandchild of a Jew, except for a person who has been a Jew and has voluntarily changed his religion.

(b) It shall be immaterial whether or not a Jew by whose right a right under subsection (a) is claimed is still alive and whether or not he has immigrated to Israel.

(c) The restrictions and conditions prescribed in respect of a Jew or an *oleh* by or under this Law or by the enactments referred to in subsection (a) shall also apply to a person who claims a right under subsection (a).

Definition.

4B. For the purposes of this Law, "Jew" means a person who was born of a Jewish mother or has become converted to Judaism and who is not a member of another religion.".

Amendment of
section 5.

2.　In section 5 of the Law of Return, 5710—1950, the following shall be added at the end: "Regulations for the purposes of sections 4A and 4B require the approval of the Constitution, Legislation and Juridical Committee of the Knesset.".

Amendment of
the Population
Registry Law,
5725-1965.

3.　In the Population Registry Law, 5725—1965 [3]), the following section shall be inserted after section 3 :

"Power of
registration
and definition.

3A. (a) A person shall not be registered as a Jew by ethnic affiliation or religion if a notification under this Law or another entry in the Registry or a public

---

*) Passed by the Knesset on 2nd Adar Bet, 5730 (10th March, 1970) and published in *Sefer Ha-Chukkim* No. 586 of the 11th Adar Bet, 5730 (19th March, 1970), p. 34 ; the Bill and an Explanatory Note were published in *Hatza'ot Chok* No. 866 of 5730, p. 36.

[1])　*Sefer Ha-Chukkim* of 5710 p. 159 — *LSI* vol. IV, p. 114 ; *Sefer Ha-Chukkim* No. 5714, p. 174 — *LSI* vol. VIII, p. 144.

[2])　*Sefer Ha-Chukkim* of 5712, p. 146 ; *LSI* vol. VI, p. 50.

[3])　*Sefer Ha-Chukkim* of 5725, p. 270 ; *LSI* vol. XIX, p. 288.

28

document indicates that he is not a Jew, so long as the said notification, entry or document has not been controverted to the satisfaction of the Chief Registration Officer or so long as declaratory judgment of a competent court or tribunal has not otherwise determined.

(b) For the purposes of this Law and of any registration or document thereunder, "Jew" has the same meaning as in section 4B of the Law of Return, 5710—1950.

(c) This section shall not derogate from a registration effected before its coming into force.".

GOLDA MEIR
Prime Minister

GOLDA MEIR
Prime Minister
Acting Minister of
the Interior

SHNEUR ZALMAN SHAZAR
President of the State

No. 32

NATIONALITY LAW, 5712—1952*

PART ONE: ACQUISITION OF NATIONALITY

Preliminary.

1. Israel nationality is acquired —
by return (section 2),
by residence in Israel (section 3),
by birth (section 4) or
by naturalisation (section 5 to 9).

There shall be no Israel nationality save under this Law.

Nationality by return.

2. (a) Every '*oleh*** under the Law of Return, 5710—1950²), shall become an Israel national.

(b) Israel nationality by return is acquired—

(1) by a person who came as an '*oleh* into, or was born in, the country before the establishment of the State — with effect from the day of the establishment of the State;

(2) by a person having come to Israel as an '*oleh* after the establishment of the State — with effect from the day of his '*aliyah***;

(3) by a person born in Israel after the establishment of the State — with effect from the day of his birth;

(4) by a person who has received an '*oleh*'s certificate under section 3 of the Law of Return, 5710—1950 — with effect from the day of the issue of the certificate.

(c) This section does not apply—

(1) to a person having ceased to be an inhabitant of Israel before the coming into force of this Law;

(2) to a person of full age who, immediately before the day of the coming into force of this Law or, if he comes to Israel as an '*oleh* thereafter, im-

---

1) *P.G.* No. 652 of the 14th December, 1936, Suppl. I, p. 285 (English Edition).

* Passed by the Knesset on the 6th Nisan, 5712 (1st April, 1952), and published in *Sefer Ha-Chukkim* No. 95 of the 13th Nisan, 5712 (8th April, 1952), p. 146; the Bill was published in *Hatza'ot Chok* No. 93 of the 22nd Cheshvan, 5712 (21st November 1951), p. 22.

** Translator's Note: '*oleh* and '*aliyah* mean respectively a Jew immigrating, and the immigration of a Jew, into the Land of Israel.

2) *Sefer Ha-Chukkim* No. 51 of the 21st Tammuz, 5710 (6th July, 1950), p. 159.

50

Reproduced from the Laws of the State of Israel, *Vol. 6 (5712–1951/52), pp. 50–53.*

mediately before the day of his *'aliyah* or the day of the issue of his *'oleh*'s certificate is a foreign national and who, on or before such day, declares that he does not desire to become an Israel national;

(3) to a minor whose parents have made a declaration under paragraph (2) and included him therein.

3. (a) A person who, immediately before the establishment of the State, was a Palestinian citizen and who does not become an Israel national under section 2, shall become an Israel national with effect from the day of the establishment of the State if —

(1) he was registered on the 4th Adar, 5712 (1st March 1952) as an inhabitant under the Registration of Inhabitants Ordinance, 5709—1949[1]); and

(2) he is an inhabitant of Israel on the day of the coming into force of this Law; and

(3) he was in Israel, or in an area which became Israel territory after the establishment of the State, from the day of the establishment of the State to the day of the coming into force of this Law, or entered Israel legally during that period.

(b) A person born after the establishment of the State who is an inhabitant of Israel on the day of the coming into force of this Law, and whose father or mother becomes an Israel national under subsection (a), shall become an Israel national with effect from the day of his birth.

4. A person born while his father or mother is an Israel national shall be an Israel national from birth; where a person is born after his father's death, it shall be sufficient that his father was an Israel national at the time of his death.

5. (a) A person of full age, not being an Israel national, may obtain Israel nationality by naturalisation if —

(1) he is in Israel; and

(2) he has been in Israel for three years out of five years preceding the day of the submission of his application; and

(3) he is entitled to reside in Israel permanently; and

(4) he has settled, or intends to settle, in Israel; and

(5) he has some knowledge of the Hebrew language; and

(6) he has renounced his prior nationality or has proved that he will cease to be a foreign national upon becoming an Israel national.

(b) Where a person has applied for naturalisation, and he meets the requirements of subsection (a), the Minister of the Interior, if he thinks fit to do so, shall grant him Israel nationality by the issue of a certificate of naturalisation.

(c) Prior to the grant of nationality, the applicant shall make the following declaration:

"I declare that I will be a loyal national of the State of Israel."

(d) Nationality is acquired on the day of the declaration.

6. (a) (1) A person who has served in the regular service of the Defence Army of Israel or who, after the 16th Kislev, 5708 (29th November, 1947) has served in some other service which the Minister of Defence, by declaration published in *Reshumot*, has declared to be military service for the purpose of this section, and who has been duly discharged from such service; and

Nationality by residence in Israel.

Nationality by birth.

Naturalisation.

Exemption from conditions of naturalisation.

---

1) *I.R.* No. 48 of the 5th Shevat, 5709 (4th February, 1949), Suppl. I, p. 164.

(2) a person who has lost a son or daughter in such service,
are exempt from the requirements of section 5 (a), except the requirement of section 5 (a) (4).

(b) A person applying for naturalisation after having made a declaration under section 2 (c) (2) is exempt from the requirement of section 5 (a) (2).

(c) A person who immediately before the establishment of the State was a Palestinian citizen is exempt from the requirement of section 5 (a) (5).

(d) The Minister of the Interior may exempt an applicant from all or any of the requirements of section 5 (a) (1), (2), (5) and (6) if there exists in his opinion a special reason justifying such exemption.

Naturalisation of husband and wife.
7. The spouse of a person who is an Israel national or who has applied for Israel nationality and meets or is exempt from the requirements of section 5 (a) may obtain Israel nationality by naturalisation even if she or he is a minor or does not meet the requirements of section (5) (a).

Naturalisation of minors.
8. Naturalisation confers Israel nationality also upon the minor children of the naturalised person.

Grant of nationality to minors.
9. (a) Where a minor, not being an Israel national, is an inhabitant of Israel, and his parents are not in Israel or have died or are unknown, the Minister of the Interior, on such conditions and with effect from such day as he may think fit, may grant him Israel nationality by the issue of a certificate of naturalisation.

(b) Nationality may be granted as aforesaid upon the application of the father or mother of the minor or, if they have died or are unable to apply, upon the application of the guardian or person in charge of the minor.

PART TWO: LOSS OF NATIONALITY

Renunciation of nationality.
10. (a) An Israel national of full age, not being an inhabitant of Israel, may declare that he desires to renounce his Israel nationality; such renunciation is subject to the consent of the Minister of the Interior; the declarant's Israel nationality terminates on the day fixed by the Minister.

(b) The Israel nationality of a minor, not being an inhabitant of Israel, terminates upon his parents' renouncing their Israel nationality; it does not terminate so long as one of his parents remains an Israel national.

Revocation of naturalisation.
11. (a) Where a person, having acquired Israel nationality by naturalisation —
(1) has done so on the basis of false particulars; or
(2) has been abroad for seven consecutive years and has no effective connection with Israel, and has failed to prove that his effective connection with Israel was severed otherwise than by his own volition; or
(3) has committed an act of disloyalty towards the State of Israel,
a District Court may, upon the application of the Minister of the Interior, revoke such person's naturalisation.

(b) The Court may, upon such application, rule that the revocation shall apply also to such children of the naturalised person as acquired Israel nationality by virtue of his naturalisation and are inhabitants of a foreign country.

(c) Israel nationality terminates on the day on which the judgment revoking naturalisation ceases to be appealable or on such later day as the Court may fix.

Saving of liability.
12. Loss of Israel nationality does not relieve from a liability arising out of such nationality and created before its loss.

102

PART THREE: FURTHER PROVISIONS

13. In this Law —

"of full age" means of the age of eighteen years or over;

"minor" means a person under eighteen years of age;

"child" includes an adopted child, and "parents" includes adoptive parents;

"foreign nationality" includes foreign citizenship, and "foreign national" includes a foreign citizen, but does not include a Palestinian citizen.

Interpretation.

14. (a) Save for the purposes of naturalisation, acquisition of Israel nationality is not conditional upon renunciation of a prior nationality.

(b) An Israel national who is also a foreign national shall, for the purposes of Israel law, be considered an Israel national.

(c) An inhabitant of Israel residing abroad shall, for the purposes of this Law, be considered an inhabitant of Israel so long as he has not settled abroad.

Dual nationality and dual residence.

15. An Israel national may obtain from the Minister of the Interior a certificate attesting his Israel nationality.

Evidence of nationality.

16. A person who knowingly gives false particulars as to a matter affecting his own or another person's acquisition or loss of Israel nationality is liable to imprisonment for a term not exceeding six months or to fine not exceeding five hundred pounds, or to both such penalties.

Offence.

17. (a) The Minister of the Interior is charged with the implementation of this Law and may make regulations as to any matter relating to its implementation, including the payment of fees and exemption from the payment thereof.

(b) The Minister of Justice may make regulations as to proceedings in District Courts under this Law, including appeals from decisions of such Courts.

Implementation and regulations.

18. (a) The Palestinian Citizenship Orders, 1925—1942[1]), are repealed with effect from the day of the establishment of the State.

(b) Any reference in any provision of law to Palestinian citizenship or Palestinian citizens shall henceforth be read as a reference to Israel nationality or Israel nationals.

(c) Any act done in the period between the establishment of the State and the day of the coming into force of this Law shall be deemed to be valid if it were valid had this Law been in force at the time it was done.

Repeal, adaptation of laws and validation.

19. (a) This Law shall come into force on the 21st Tammuz, 5712 (14th July, 1952).

(b) Even before that day, the Minister of the Interior may make regulations as to declarations under section 2 (c) (2).

Commencement.

MOSHE SHARETT
Minister of Foreign Affairs

MOSHE SHAPIRA
Minister of the Interior

YOSEF SPRINZAK
Chairman of the Knesset
Acting President of the State

---

1) *Palestine Gazette* No. 1210 of the 16th July, 1942, Suppl. II, p. 1193 (English Edition).

(No. 26)

NATIONALITY (AMENDMENT) LAW, 5718—1958*

1. Section 10 of the Nationality Law, 5712—1952[1]), shall be replaced by the following section :

Replacement of section 10.

"Renunciation of nationality.

10. (a) An Israel national of full age, not being an inhabitant of Israel, may declare that he desires to renounce his Israel nationality.

(b) An Israel national of full age who declares that he desires to cease being an inhabitant of Israel may, if the Minister of the Interior considers that there is a special reason justifying it declare that he desires to renounce his Israel nationality.

(c) Every remuneration of Israel nationality is subject to the consent of the Minister of the Interior.

(d) Where the Minister of the Interior has consented to the renunciation, Israel nationality shall terminate on the day fixed by the Minister.

(e) The Israel nationality of a minor terminates upon his parents' renouncing their Israel nationality, but where the parents have renounced their Israel nationality under subsection (b), the Minister of the Interior may, if he considers that there is a special reason justifying it, refuse to consent to the renunciation in so far as it concerns the termination of the minor's Israel nationality.

(f) The Israel nationality of a minor shall not terminate by virtue of this section so long as one of his parents remains an Israel national.".

DAVID BEN-GURION   ISRAEL BAR-YEHUDA
Prime Minister   *Minister of the Interior*

YITZCHAK BEN-ZVI
President of the State

---

*   Passed by the Knesset on the 11th Adar 5718 (3rd March, 1958) and published in *Sefer Ha-Chukkim* No. 246 of the 21st Adar, 5718 (13th March, 1958), p. 84; the Bill and an Explanatory Note were published in *Hatza'ot Chok* No. 337 of 5718, p. 160.

[1])   *Sefer Ha-Chukkim* No. 95 of 5712. p. 146; *LSI* vol. VI, p. 50.

Reproduced from the Laws of the State of Israel, *Vol. 12 (5718–1957/58). p. 99.*

(No. 50)

NATIONALITY (AMENDMENT NO. 2) LAW, 5728—1968 *

1.   In section 1 of the Nationality Law, 5712—1952 [1]) (hereinafter   Amendment of
referred to as "the principal Law"), the line "or by naturalisation (sec-   section 1.
tions 5 to 9)" shall be replaced by the lines :

"by birth and residence in Israel (section 4A)
by naturalisation (sections 5 to 8) or
by grant (section 9)".

2.   In section 2 of the principal Law —   Amendment of
section 2.

(1) paragraphs (2) and (3) of subsection (c) shall be replaced by
the following paragraphs :

"(2) to a person of full age who immediately before the day of
his *aliyah* or immediately before the day of the issue of his
oleh's certificate was a foreign national and who, on or before
that day or within three months thereafter and while still a
foreign national declares that he does not wish to become an
Israel national ; a person as aforesaid may, by written notice
to the Minister of the Interior, waive his right to make a declaration under this paragraph ;

(3) to a minor of foreign nationality born outside Israel whose
parents have made a declaration under paragraph (2) and included him therein ; for this purpose, a declaration by one parent
shall be sufficient if the written consent of the other parent has
been attached thereto or if the declarant is entitled to have sole
possession of the minor ;

(4) to a person born in Israel after the establishment of the
State to a diplomatic or consular representative of a foreign
state, other than an honorary representative." ;

(2) the following subsection shall be inserted after subsection (c) ;

"(d) An Israel resident on whom Israel nationality has not been
conferred by reason of a declaration under subsection (c) (3)
may, in the period between his eighteenth birthday and his
twenty-first birthday, declare that he wishes to become an Israel
national, and from the day of his declaration he shall be an
Israel national by virtue of return.".

*)   Passed by the Knesset on the 13th Av, 5728 (7th August, 1968) and pub-
lished in *Sefer Ha-Chukkim* No. 538 of the 22nd Av, 5728 (16th August,
1968), p. 212 ; the Bill and an Explanatory Note were published in *Hatza'ot
Chok* No. 707 of 5727, p. 15.

[1])   *Sefer Ha-Chukkim* of 5712, p. 146 — *LSI* vol. VI, p. 50 ; *Sefer Ha-
Chukkim* of 5718, p. 84 — *LSI* vol. XII, p. 99.

(No. 42)

NATIONALITY (AMENDMENT No. 3) LAW, 5731-1971*

1.   In the Nationality Law, 5712-1952[1], the following subsection shall be added at the end of section 2 :

Amendment of section 2.

"(e)   Where a person has expressed his desire to settle in Israel, being a person who has received, or is entitled to receive, an *oleh*'s** visa under the Law of Return, 5710-1950[2], the Minister of the Interior may at his discretion, grant him, upon his application, nationality by virtue of return even before his *aliya***.".

GOLDA MEIR
Prime Minister

YOSEF BURG
Minister of the Interior

SHNEUR ZALMAN SHAZAR
President of the State

---

*   Passed by the Knesset on the 22nd Iyar, 5731 (17th May, 1971) and published in *Sefer Ha-Chukkim* No. 624 of the 2nd Sivan, 5731 (26th May, 1971), p. 118; the Bill and an Explanatory Note were published in *Hatza'ot Chok* No. 935 of 5731, p. 192.

**   *Oleh* and *aliya* mean an immigrant, and immigration, under the Law of Return, 5710-1950.

1)   *Sefer Ha-Chukkim* of 5712, p. 146 — *LSI* vol. VI, p. 50; *Sefer Ha-Chukkim* of 5718, p. 84 — *LSI* vol. XII, p. 99; *Sefer Ha-Chukkim* of 5728, p. 212 — *LSI* vol. XXII, p. 241.

2)   *Sefer Ha-Chukkim* of 5710, p. 159; *LSI* vol. IV, p. 114.

Reproduced from the Laws of the State of Israel, *Vol. 25 (5731–1970/71). p. 117.*

No. 64

RABBINICAL COURTS JURISDICTION (MARRIAGE AND DIVORCE) LAW, 5713—1953°

1. Matters of marriage and divorce of Jews in Israel, being nationals or residents of the State, shall be under the exclusive jurisdiction of rabbinical courts.

Jurisdiction in matters of marriage and divorce.

2. Marriages and divorces of Jews shall be performed in Israel in accordance with Jewish religious law.

Performance of marriages and divorces.

3. Where a suit for divorce between Jews has been filed in a rabbinical court, whether by the wife or by the husband, a rabbinical court shall have exclusive jurisdiction in any matter connected with such suit, including maintenance for the wife and for the children of the couple.

Jurisdiction in matters incidental to divorce.

4. Where a Jewish wife sues her Jewish husband or his estate for maintenance in a rabbinical court, otherwise than in connection with divorce, the plea of the defendant that a rabbinical court has no jurisdiction in the matter shall not be heard.

Jurisdiction in matters of maintenance.

5. Where a woman sues her deceased husband's brother for *chalitza*[1]) in a rabbinical court, the rabbinical court shall have exclusive jurisdiction in the matter, also as regards maintenance for the woman until the day on which *chalitza* is given.

Jurisdiction in matters of *chalitza*.

'6. Where a rabbinical court, by final judgment, has ordered that a husband be compelled to grant his wife a letter of divorce or that a wife be compelled to accept a letter of divorce from her husband, a district court may, upon expiration of six months from the day of the making of the order, on the application of the Attorney General, compel compliance with the order by imprisonment.

Compelling the grant or acceptance of a letter of divorce.

7. Where a rabbinical court, by final judgment, has ordered that a man be compelled to give his brother's widow *chalitza*, a district court may, upon expiration of three months from the day of the making of the order, on application of the Attorney General, compel compliance with the order by imprisonment.

Compelling the giving of *chalitza*.

---

* Passed by the Knesset on the 15th Elul, 5713 (26th August, 1953) and published in *Sefer Ha-Chukkim* No. 134 of the 24th Elul, 5713 (4th September, 1953), p. 165; the Bill and an Explanatory Note were published in *Hatza'ot Chok* No. 163 of the 27th Iyar, 5713 (12th May, 1953), p. 186.

1) Performance of the ceremony releasing him from the duty of marrying her (Tr.)

Reproduced from the Laws of the State of Israel, *Vol. 7 (5713–1952/53), pp. 139–40.*

Finality of judgment.

8. For the purpose of sections 6 and 7, a judgment shall be regarded as final when it is no longer appealable.

Jurisdiction by consent.

9. In matters of personal status of Jews, as specified in article 51 of the Palestine Orders in Council, 1922 to 1947, or in the Succession Ordinance, in which a rabbinical court has not exclusive jurisdiction under this Law, a rabbinical court shall have jurisdiction after all parties concerned have expressed their consent thereto.

Validity of judgments.

10. A judgment given by a rabbinical court after the establishment of the State and before the coming into force of this Law, after the case had been heard in the presence of the litigants, and which would have been validly given had this Law been in force at the time, shall be deemed to have been validly given.

Implementation.

11. The Minister of Religious Affairs is charged with the implementation of this Law.

MOSHE SHARETT
Minister of Foreign Affairs
Acting Prime Minister

MOSHE SHAPIRA
Minister of Religious Affairs

YITZCHAK BEN-ZVI
President of the State

(No. 83)

MATTERS OF DISSOLUTION OF MARRIAGE (JURISDICTION IN SPECIAL CASES) LAW, 5729-1969*

Power of
President of
Supreme Court.

1.　(a)　Matters of dissolution of marriage which are not within the exclusive jurisdiction of a religious court shall be within the jurisdiction of the District Court or a religious court, as the President of the Supreme Court may determine.

(b)　This Law shall not apply where both spouses are Jews, Muslims, Druze or members of one of the Christian communities which maintain a religious court in Israel.

Preliminary
clarification.

2.　(a)　Where one of the spouses is a Jew, a Muslim, a Druze, or a member of one of the Christian communities which maintain a religious court in Israel, the President of the Supreme Court shall not exercise his power under section 1 until he has received an opinion from a religious court as provided in this section.

(b)　The Attorney-General or his representative shall apply in writing to the religious court concerned or to each of the two religious courts concerned, describing the circumstances of the case and requesting a written opinion as to whether, in the circumstances described, the religious court would perform or grant a divorce, or annul the marriage or declare it void *ab initio*, and the religious court shall give the opinion as requested.

(c)　When the requested opinion has been given, the Attorney-General shall submit it to the President of the Supreme Court, who, after perusing the opinion, shall at his discretion decide whether to refer the matter to a religious court or to the District Court.

Restriction on
determination
of jurisdiction.

3.　The President of the Supreme Court may refrain from determining jurisdiction under this Law if he is of the opinion that in the circumstances of the case the applicant should not be granted relief.

Inapplicable
provisions.

4.　(a)　Article 55 of the Palestine Order in Council, 1922-1947[1]), shall not apply to a matter dealt with by this Law.

(b)　The provisos in article 64(1)·and in the second sentence of article 65 of the said Order in Council shall not apply to a matter in respect of which jurisdiction is determined under this Law.

Choice of
law in
District
Court.

5.　(a)　The District Court vested with jurisdiction under this Law shall apply one of the undermentioned to the matter, in the following order of preference :

---

*　Passed by the Knesset on the 2nd Av, 5729 (17th July, 1969) and published in *Sefer Ha-Chukkim* No. 573 of the 12th Av, 5729 (27th July, 1969), p. 109; the Bill and an Explanatory Note were published in *Hatza'ot Chok* No. 813 of 5729, p. 109.

1)　*Laws of Palestine* vol. III, p. 2569 (English Edition).

Reproduced from the Laws of the State of Israel, *Vol. 23 (5729-1968/69), pp. 274-75.*

(1) the domestic law of the common domicile of the spouses;

(2) the domestic law of the last common domicile of the spouses;

(3) the domestic law of the country of which both spouses are nationals;

(4) the domestic law of the place where the marriage was contracted :

Provided that the Court shall not deal with the matter in accordance with any such law as aforesaid if different rules would apply thereunder to the two spouses.

(b) In the absence of any law applicable under subsection (a), the Court may apply the domestic law of the domicile of one of the spouses, as it may deem just in the circumstances of the case.

(c) Consent of the spouses shall always be a ground for divorce.

6. In this Law —   Definitions.

"dissolution of marriage" includes divorce, annulment of marriage and declaration of a marriage as void *ab initio;*

"religious court" means a rabbinical court, a Sharia court, a religious court of a Christian community and a Druze religious court, all within the respective meanings assigned to these terms by law;

"domicile" has the meaning assigned to this term by section 80 of the Capacity and Guardianship Law, 5722-1962[1]).

7. The Minister of Justice may make regulations as to the proceed-   Regulations.
ings before the President of the Supreme Court and as to the request of the Attorney-General or his representative for an opinion of a religious court under this Law.

8. The provisions of this Law shall not derogate from section 9 of   Saving of
the Rabbinical Courts Jurisdiction (Marriage and Divorce) Law, 5713-   laws.
1953[2]), or from section 18 of the Courts Law, 5717-1957[3]).

GOLDA MEIR   GOLDA MEIR
Prime Minister   *Prime Minister*
                               Acting Minister of Justice

SHNEUR ZALMAN SHAZAR
President of the State

---

1) *Sefer Ha-Chukkim* of 5722, p. 120; *LSI* vol. XVI, p. 106.
2) *Sefer Ha-Chukkim* of 5713, p. 165; *LSI* vol. VII, p. 139.
3) *Sefer Ha-Chukkim* of 5717, p. 148; *LSI* vol. XI, p. 157.

(No. 67)

POPULATION REGISTRY LAW, 5725–1965 *

Chapter One : Registry

Interpretation
and applicability.

1.   (a)   In this Law, "resident" means a person who is in Israel as an Israel national or under an *oleh*'s [1]) visa or *oleh*'s certificate or under a permit of permanent residence.

(b)   Any other person who is in Israel, except a person who is therein under a permit of transitory residence or a visitor's permit of residence or under a foreign diplomatic passport, shall, for the purposes of this Law, be likewise regarded as a resident.

(c)   The provisions of this Law conferring rights or imposing duties on, or relating to, a resident shall apply also to an Israel national who is not a resident.

Registry and
particulars of
registration.

2.   (a)   The following particulars relating to a resident, and any change therein, shall be entered in the Population Registry :

      (1)   Surname, first name and previous names;

      (2)   names of parents;

---

*   Passed by the Knesset on the 22nd Tammuz, 5725 (22nd July, 1965) and published in *Sefer Ha-Chukkim* No. 466 of the 3rd Av, 5725 (1st August, 1965), p. 270; the Bill and an Explanatory Note were published in *Hatza'ot Chok* No. 622 of 5724, p. 266.

[1])   *Oleh* — an immigrant by virtue of the Law of Return, 5710–1950 (Tr.).

Reproduced from the Laws of the State of Israel, *Vol. 19 (5725–1964/65), pp. 288–97.*

(3)   date and place of birth;

(4)   sex;

(5)   ethnic group;

(6)   religion;

(7)   personal status (single, maried, divorced or widowed);

(8)   name of spouse;

(9)   names, dates of birth, and sex, of children;

(10) past and present nationality or nationalities;

(11) address;

(12) date of entry into Israel;

(13) date of becoming a resident, within the meaning of sub-section 1 (a).

(b)   When a resident is first registered, an "identity number" shall be fixed for his registration.

3.   The entry in the Registry and any copy thereof or extract therefrom, and any certificate issued under this Law, shall be *prima facie* evidence of the correctness of the particulars of registration referred to in paragraphs (1) to (4) and (9) to (13) of section 2.

Registry to be *prima facie* evidence.

4.   The Minister of the Interior shall appoint a Chief Registration Officer and registration officers for the keeping of the Registry in accordance with the provisions of this Law.

Registration officers.

Chapter Two : Notification

5.   Every resident shall notify a registration officer, within thirty days from the day on which he first entered Israel or, if he became a resident after entering Israel, from the day on which he became a resident, of his particulars of registration, within the meaning of section 2; and if at the time of entering or becoming a resident he had charge of a minor or of a person of full age incapable of fulfilling his duty under this section, he shall notify also the particulars of registration of such minor or person of full age.

Duty to notify particulars of registration.

6.   Notification of a birth which occurred in Israel shall be made to a registration officer within ten days. It shall be made by the person in charge of the institution at which the birth occurred or, if the birth did not occur in an institution, by the parents of the child and by the physician and midwife who attended to the birth. The notification shall contain the particulars of registration of the child and such other particulars as shall be prescribed by regulations with the approval of the Home Affairs Committee of the Knesset.

Notification of birth in Israel.

7.   Notification of a death which occurred in Israel shall be made within 48 hours to a registration officer or to the person empowered to

Notification of death in Israel.

*A Section 3A was added pursuant to Law of Return (Amendment No. 2), 5730–1970, Laws of the State of Israel, *Vol. 24 (5730–1969/70), pp. 28–29.*

issue the burial permit under the Public Health Ordinance, 1940 [1]). It shall be made by the person in charge of the institution in which the death occurred or by the physician who ascertained the death or, in the absence of a physician, by a person who was present at the time of death. The notification shall contain the particulars of registration of the deceased and such other particulars as shall be prescribed by regulations with the approval of the Home Affairs Committee of the Knesset.

Definition of "institution".

8.   For the purposes of sections 6 and 7, "institution" includes a hospital, a prison, a public or religious institution, a charitable institution, a home, within the meaning of the Homes (Supervision) Law, 5725–1965 [2]), and a hotel; and a public vehicle, vessel or aircraft shall be deemed to be an institution.

Foundling.

9.   Where an infant is found abandoned, any person first obtaining possession of the infant shall within ten days make notification to a registration officer of such particulars of registration of the infant as are known to him and transmit to him any such other information as he may have concerning the birth of the infant.

Discovery of dead body.

10.   Where the police have been notified of the discovery of a dead body, under section 21 of the Criminal Procedure Amendment (Investigation of Felonies and Causes of Death) Law, 5718–1958 [3]), they shall transmit to a registration officer any information they may possess concerning the particulars of registration of the deceased.

Birth abroad.

11.   A resident to whom a child is born abroad shall within thirty days make notification to the registration officer of the particulars of registration of the child.

Death abroad.

12.   Where a resident dies abroad, his spouse, or a child or parent of his, being a resident, shall make notification of the fact to a registration officer within thirty days from the day on which the death comes to his knowledge.

Adoption abroad.

13.   A resident who adopts a child abroad shall within thirty days make notification to a registration officer of the particulars of registration of the child and transmit to the registration officer the document of adoption; the same applies, *mutatis mutandis,* where the adoption of a child is rescinded abroad.

Leaving Israel.

14.   A resident of full age who leaves Israel with a view to settling abroad shall notify the registration officer of the fact. The notification shall include also his minor children who leave with him.

[1])   *P. G.* of 1940, Suppl. I, No. 1065, p. 239 (English Edition); *Sefer Ha-Chukkim* of 5722, p. 12 — *LSI* vol. XVI, p. 10.

[2])   *Sefer Ha-Chukkim* of 5725, p. 48; *supra,* p. 44.

[3])   *Sefer Ha-Chukkim* of 5718, p. 54; *LSI* vol. XII, p. 66.

15. In the event of any of the following acts, the authority concerned shall deliver to a registration officer, within fourteen days from the date of the act, a copy of the document attesting it, accompanied by such particulars specified in regulations as are necessary for the identification of the person concerned :

(1) Change of name, choice of name or fixing of name under the Names Law, 5716–1956 [1]);

(2) a marriage registered under the Marriage and Divorce (Registration) Ordinance [2]) ;

(3) a change of religion registered under the Religious Community (Change) Ordinance [3]);

(4) naturalisation or renunciation of nationality under the Nationality Law, 5712–1952 [4]) ;

(5) a notification of death under section 7 to the person empowered to issue the burial permit.

Delivery of documents of official acts.

16. Where a civil or religious court has given a decision declaring a change in the particulars of registration of any person or a decision involving a change as aforesaid, it shall deliver a copy of such decision to the Chief Registration Officer. The same shall be done in respect of a copy of an adoption order, divorce certificate or declaration of death.

Delivery of copies of judgments and declarations.

17. Where a change other than as referred to in section 15 or 16 occurs in the particulars of registration of any resident, such resident shall within thirty days make notification of the change to the registration officer; and where a resident has charge of a minor or a person of full age incapable of fulfilling his duty under this section, such resident shall within thirty days make notification of any change as aforesaid in the particulars of registration of such minor or person of full age.

Duty to notify changes.

18. (a) Notification under any of the sections of this chapter by one of those required to make it shall release the others from the duty of notification.

Release from duty of notification.

(b) A notification under section 7 containing particulars of the spouse of a deceased person shall release such spouse from the duty of notifying her or his widowed state.

CHAPTER THREE: POWERS OF REGISTRATION OFFICER

19. A registration officer may demand from a person making notification under Chapter Two or from any other person required to make that notification — even if he has become released by virtue of section 18 or the period prescribed for making the notification has passed —

Demand for information and declarations.

[1]) *Sefer Ha-Chukkim* of 5716, p. 94; *LSI* vol. **X**, p. 95.
[2]) *Laws of Palestine* vol. II, cap. 88, p. 903 (English Edition).
[3]) *Laws of Palestine* vol. II, cap. 127, p. 1294 (English Edition).
[4]) *Sefer Ha-Chukkim* of 5712, p. 146; *LSI* vol. **VI**, p. 50.

(1) to furnish him with any information or document in his possession concerning the particulars of the registration to which the notification relates, unless the information or document is calculated to incriminate him;

(2) to make a written or oral declaration of the correctness of any document or information furnished by him.

Registration of adoption.

20. Where a child has been adopted, then, in the Registry and in any document under this Law, the adopters shall be registered as his parents and the adoptee as their child, under the name fixed for him in the adoption order.

Name of father where woman unmarried.

21. The name of the father of the child of an unmarried mother shall be registered on the basis of a joint notification by the father and the mother or on the basis of a judgment of a competent civil or religious court.

Name of father where mother married.

22. Save under a judgment of a competent civil or religious court, a man shall not be registered as the father of the child of a woman who had been married to another man within 300 days prior to the date of the birth of the child.

Correction of clerical errors.

23. The Chief Registration Officer may direct the correction of a clerical error or omission which occurred in the Registry or in any document issued under this Law.

CHAPTER FOUR : IDENTITY CERTIFICATE

Right to receive identity certificate.

24. A resident who is in Israel and who has completed his sixteenth year may receive an identity certificate. A resident who is in Israel and who has not completed his sixteenth year may receive an identity certificate with the consent of his representative, within the meaning of section 80 of the Capacity and Guardianship Law, 5722–1962 [1]), or with the approval of the Chief Registration Officer.

Contents of identity certificate.

25. An identity certificate shall contain the particulars of registration prescribed by the Minister of the Interior with the approval of the Constitution, Legislation and Juridical Committee of the Knesset. The names of the children shall be entered both in the identity certificate of their father and in the identity certificate of their mother. A photograph of the holder shall be attached to every certificate, except the certificate of a woman who declares that she refuses to be photographed for religious reasons. An identity certificate shall bear the signature or fingerprint of the holder.

Period of validity of identity certificate.

26. The period of validity of an identity certificate shall be seven years from the date of issue.

[1]) *Sefer Ha-Chukkim* of 5722, p. 120; *LSI* vol. XVI, p. 106.

27.   Nothing shall be entered in an identity certificate otherwise than in accordance with a provision of a Law or of regulations made by the Minister of the Interior.

Prohibition of entry in identity certificate.

28.   (a)   A registration officer may require the holder of a certificate to submit it for the purpose of entering a change in a particular of registration or if the certificate is worn out or has expired or if the photograph no longer correctly represents the holder.

Power to call in identity certificate.

(b)   Where in dealing with an identity certificate it appears to a registration officer that any change, correction, addition or deletion has been made therein unlawfully, he may retain such identity certificate until the matter has been fully examined.

Chapter Five : Receipt of Information

29.   (a)   Any person may receive information concerning, or a copy of or extract from, the entry in the Registry relating to him.

Information.

(b)   Any person may receive information concerning the name and address of any other person registered in the Registry.

(c)   A person who is *prima facie* interested may receive information as to the date of birth, and other particulars of registration determined by regulations, of a person registered in the Registry.

30.   (a)   A person born in Israel who is registered in the Registry may receive a birth certificate.

Birth and death certificates.

(b)   A person who is *prima facie* interested may receive a birth certificate or death certificate of another person registered in the register if the birth or death took place in Israel.

31.   The Registry and the documents therein shall not be open for inspection except to the following for the purpose of the discharge of their duties:

Inspection of Registry.

(1)   The Minister of the Interior or a person empowered by him in that behalf;

(2)   the Minister of Defence or a person empowered by him in that behalf;

(3)   the Attorney General or his representative;

(4)   the Inspector-General of Police or a person empowered by him in that behalf;

(5)   a person empowered in that behalf by a civil or religious court for the purposes of a specific matter pending before it;

(6)   a marriage registrar or a person empowered in that behelf by a marriage registrar.

32.   Sections 29 to 31 shall not derogate from the provisions of section 27 of the Adoption of Children Law, 5720–1960 [1]), and particulars

Information as to adoption.

---

[1])   *Sefer Ha-Chukkim* of 5720, p. 96; *LSI* vol. **XIV**, p. 93.

likely to lead to the identification of an adopter or an adoptee or his parents or other relatives shall not be disclosed except to the persons specified in that section. The Minister of the Interior shall issue directions aimed at enabling a marriage registrar, or a particular person who requires such information for the discharge of his duties in the registration of marriages, to ascertain whether a particular candidate for marriage is an adoptee.

CHAPTER SIX : OFFENCES

Criminal use of identity certificate.

33.   Any person who —

(1)   delivers his identity certificate or part thereof to another person for an illegal purpose; or

(2)   unlawfully alters, corrects, adds or deletes any entry in an identity certificate; or

(3)   wilfully destroys an identity certificate or part thereof;

shall be liable to imprisonment for a term of one year.

Possession of identity certificate in which alteration has been made.

34.   A person who kept possession of his identity certificate after any unlawful alteration, correction, addition or deletion had been made therein, and who does not prove that he did so in good faith, shall be liable to imprisonment for a term of six months.

Various offences.

35.   (a)   A person who discloses the contents of the directions of the Minister of the Interior referred to in section 32 to a person other than a marriage registrar or a person requiring the knowledge of those directions for the discharge of his functions in the registration of marriages shall, if he is a public servant, be liable to imprisonment for a term of three years or, if he is not a public servant, be liable to imprisonment for a term of three months.

(b)   Any person who —

(1)   for his identification produces the identity certificate of another person as if it were his own identity certificate; or

(2)   for the purposes of this Law delivers any information, document or notification knowing it to be incorrect; or

(3)   unlawfully refuses a demand of a registration officer under section 19; or

(4)   having been required by a registration officer to submit his identity certificate in accordance with section 28 (a), does not do so within the time prescribed in the requisition

shall be liable to imprisonment for a term of three months.

(c)   A person who does not within the time prescribed deliver any notification which he is bound to deliver under sections 5–7, 9, 11–13 and 17 shall be liable to imprisonment for a term of two weeks or to a fine of 100 pounds.

36. In section 2 of the Penal Law Amendment (Offences Committed Abroad) Law, 5716–1955 [1]), the following paragraph shall be inserted after paragraph (8) :

"(9) an offence under the Population Registry Law, 5725–1965.".

Amendment of
Penal Law
Amendment
(Offences Com-
mitted Abroad)
Law.

CHAPTER SEVEN : MISCELLANEOUS

37. The Minister of the Interior may make regulations as to the renewal of such entries in the Registry, a register of births or a register of deaths as have been lost or destroyed. For the purposes of renewal as aforesaid, every person concerned shall, as far as possible, be given an opportunity to be heard.

Renewal of
lost entries.

38. The Minister of the Interior may, by order, empower a local authority to carry out any function under this Law.

Assignment of
functions to
local authority.

39. (a) The Minister of the Interior may, with the consent of the Minister of Health, make regulations as to anything relating to the registration of births and deaths, including regulations concerning —

(1) the forms for the notification of births and deaths;

(2) the form of registers of births and deaths;

(3) the form of certificates of births and deaths;

(4) the late registration of births and deaths, including the birth of residents born in Cyprus or Mauritius who immigrated into Israel on or before the 29th Elul, 5709 (23rd September, 1949).

(b) Regulations under subsection (a) concerning births and deaths which occur in vessels or aircraft registered in Israel shall be made with the consent also of the Minister of Transport. Regulations concerning the registration of the death of soldiers shall be made with the consent also of the Minister of Defence.

Regulations
concerning the
registration
of births and
deaths.

40. Registration under this Law shall not affect the laws regarding prohibition and permission in matters of marriage and divorce.

Saving of laws.

41. The Minister of the Interior may exempt classes of persons from compliance with all or part of the provisions of this Law in so far as it seems necessary to him to do so for the purpose of the implementation of an international convention to which Israel is a party.

Exemption.

42. In the Public Health Ordinance, 1940 —

(1) section 4 to 6 shall be replaced by the following sections :

Amendment of
Public Health
Ordinance, 1940.

"Notification of birth of dead infant. 4. (1) Where an infant issues from his mother dead after the expiration of the twenty-eighth week of pregnancy (such an infant hereinafter referred to as a "dead

[1]) *Sefer Ha-Chukkim* of 5716, p. 7 ; *LSI* vol. X, p. 7.

infant"), the father or mother or, if they fail to fulfil this duty, the midwife or other person who attended the mother at or within six hours after the birth shall notify the birth of the dead infant. Notification shall be made within fifteen days from the date of the birth to the District Health Office or, if there is no District Health Office in the locality concerned, to a physician empowered in that behalf by the Director.

(2) A physician as referred to in subsection (1) shall keep a record of all the births of dead infants which occur in his area of jurisdiction and which are notified in accordance with subsection (1) or of which he is otherwise notified, and after recording the notifications he shall transmit them, or a copy of them, as shall be prescribed, to the nearest District Health Office.

(3) Where the birth of a dead infant is not notified through the fault of the parents or of another person obligated to notify it, a Government physician or an inspector may, at any time after the expiration of fifteen days from the date of the birth, require any person obligated to make notification under this section to give information, to the best of his knowledge and belief, of the particulars which he is obligated to notify as aforesaid, and such person shall comply with the requisition.";

(2) paragraph (d) of section 8(1) shall be replaced by the following paragraph :

"(d) A burial permit shall not be issued unless notification of the death has been made, in accordance with the Population Registry Law, 5725–1965, to the District Health Office or to a physician empowered under paragraph (b) (2), as the case may be, or to a registration officer within the meaning of the said Law, indicating, among the other particulars, the cause of death as determined by a physician and certified by his signature. Where the cause of death has not been determined by a physician, it may be determined by a physician of the District Health Office or a physician empowered under paragraph (b) (2), as the case may be, to the best of his knowledge and belief, and certified by his signature.".

Repeal.

43. The Registration of Inhabitants Ordinance, 5709–1949[1]), is hereby repealed.

Transitional provisions.

44. (a) The Register of Inhabitants kept under the Registration of Inhabitants Ordinance, 5709–1949, shall, from the coming into force of this Ordinance, be part of the Registry under this Law.

---

[1]) *I. R.* of 5709, Suppl. I, No. 48, p. 164; *LSI* vol. II, p. 103.

(b) Wherever in any provision of law reference is made to registration under the Registration of Inhabitants Ordinance, 5709–1949, such reference shall, unless the context otherwise requires, be deemed to be a reference to registration under this Law.

(c) An identification booklet issued under the Emergency Regulations (Registration of Inhabitants), 5708–1948 [1]), and an identity certificate, or any other certificate, issued under the Registration of Inhabitants Ordinance, 5709–1949, or the Public Health Ordinance, 1940, shall be deemed to be certificates under this Law.

(d) Notwithstanding anything provided in section 26, an identification booklet or identity certificate, as referred to in subsection (c), shall not expire before the expiration of three years from the date of the coming into force of this Law or before the elections to the Seventh Knesset, whichever is the later date.

45. The particulars entered in identity certificates immediately before the coming into force of this Law shall be entered in identity certificates issued during the six months immediately following the date of the coming into force of this Law, but not later than the date of the coming into force of regulations under section 25.

Temporary
provision.

46. The Minister of the Interior shall prescribe by regulations the procedure for the registration of Israel nationals who on the date of the coming into force of this Law had not been registered under the Registration of Inhabitants Ordinance, 5709–1949.

Registration
of Israel
nationals
abroad.

47. The Minister of the Interior is charged with the implementation of this Law and may, with the approval of the Constitution, Legislation and Juridical Committee of the Knesset, make regulations as to any matter relating to such implementation, including regulations as to —

Implementation
and regulations.

(1) the procedure for notifying particulars of registration and any changes therein to the Registry Offices or to Israeli Representations abroad;

(2) the places for the delivery of notifications under this Law;

(3) rules for the issue of certificates, extracts, copies and information;

(4) fees for services and certificates under this Law;

(5) the registration of the death of a person who died abroad, whose death has not been registered and who was buried in Israel;

(6) the correction of clerical errors and omissions under section 23.

48. This Law shall come into force at the expiration of one year from the date of its publication in *Reshumot*.

Commencement.

Levi Eshkol   Haim Moshe Shapira
Prime Minister   *Minister of the Interior*

Shneur Zalman Shazar
President of the State

[1]) *I. R.* of 5708, Suppl. II, No. 16, p. 77.

Notes

INTRODUCTION—HOW THE "WHO IS A JEW?" QUESTION
AROSE

1. See Salo W. Baron, "Who Is A Jew? Some Historical Reflections,"
Midstream, Vol. VI, No. 2 (Spring, 1960), pp. 5–16.

2. Law of Return, 5710–1950, *Laws of the State of Israel,* Vol. 4 (5710–
1949/50) and Nationality Law, 5712–1952, *Laws of the State of Israel,* Vol.
6 (5712–1951/52).

3. The Minister of the Interior later testified that he issued his instructions in conformity with the policy formulated by his four predecessors
and a statement of the Attorney General. *Divrei (Proceedings) HaKnesset,*
Third Knesset, 488th Session, Vol. 24 (July 28, 1958), p. 2236. The Minister
of Religious Affairs voiced the opposition of the Orthodox rabbinate when
he submitted his budget to the Knesset on March 12, 1958. *Divrei HaKnesset,* Third Knesset, 433rd Session, Vol. 23 (March 13, 1958), p. 1296. See
also Eliezer Goldman, *Religious Issues in Israel's Political Life* (Jerusalem:
Mador Dati, The Youth and he-Haluz Department of the World Zionist
Organization, 1964).

4. See *New York Times,* July 2, 1958, p. 5, and August 31, 1959, p. E7;
Israel Digest, Vol. I, No. 6 (July 11, 1958), p. 3; and *Israel Government Year
Book 5719–1958* (Jerusalem: The Government Printer, 1958), p. 17. A
central point of conflict was the problem of conversion. The Orthodox
rabbinical authorities refused to convert children of mixed marriages if the

mother was not Jewish and if she would not convert. This was consistent with Orthodox religious doctrine that a child follows the religion of the mother.

5. *Israel Digest,* Vol. I, No. 7 (July 25, 1958), p. 3.

6. Among the Jewish Americans who received Prime Minister Ben-Gurion's letter were Supreme Court Justice Felix Frankfurter, Judge Simon Rifkind, and Professor Harry A. Wolfson of Harvard University. In February, 1968 Premier Ben-Gurion's own granddaughter was caught in the legal dilemma. Ben-Gurion's son had married a Christian in England during World War II; and their daughter, when she applied to be married, had to produce documentary evidence to the Orthodox rabbinate of her mother's conversion to Judaism under Orthodox auspices. Since such documents were not presented and only Orthodox rabbis could perform marriages between Jews in Israel, no rabbi would marry the couple until proof of the conversion was furnished or Ben-Gurion's granddaughter would convert. (*New York Times,* February 23, 1968, p. 35)

7. *Israel Digest,* Vol. I, No. 17 (December 12, 1958), pp. 2–3. The official letter is reproduced in Baruch Litvin and Sidney B. Hoenig, *Jewish Identity: Modern Responsa and Opinions on The Registration of Children of Mixed Marriages* (New York: Philipp Feldheim, Inc., 1965), pp. 11–15.

8. Litvin and Hoenig, *op. cit.,* p. 13.

9. *Ibid.,* p. 14.

10. The replies published by Israel's Government on August 2, 1959 revealed that an overwhelming majority of those who answered felt that the children should be registered only on the basis of Orthodox Jewish religious law. See *Israel Digest,* Vol. II, No. 16 (August 7, 1959), p. 4.

11. *New York Times,* December 2, 1958, p. 15.

12. *Divrei HaKnesset,* Third Knesset, 685th Session, Vol. 27 (July 29, 1959), p. 2782. See Ervin Birnbaum, *The Politics of Compromise: State and Religion in Israel* (Rutherford, N.J.: Fairleigh Dickinson University Press, 1970), pp. 237–38 and 245; Ben Halpern, "Who is a Jew?," *Jewish Frontier,* Vol. XXVI, No. 1 (January 1959), pp. 7–10; and Jakob J. Petuchowsky, "Who is a Jew?," *Jewish Frontier,* Vol. XXVI, No. 6 (June 1959), pp. 6–10.

13. The Hebrew word "Halachah" literally means "The Way" and describes traditional Orthodox religious law, which consists of the Torah, or Old Testament, and the Talmud. Actually, there are two Talmuds: one, the Babylonian Talmud, written in about 500 C.E., and the other, the Palestinian Talmud, written about a hundred years earlier. Each is composed of: (1) the Mishnah, edited by Rabbi Judah the Prince in about 200 C.E., which is a compilation of brief statements of the principles, rules and laws governing all aspects of living and which constituted the oral law; and

(2) the Gemorah, which presents various leading rabbinical thinkers' commentaries on, and analyses and discussions of, the matters set in the Mishnah.

LAW OF RETURN

14. Law of Return, *supra* note 2, p. 114.

15. Law of Return (Amendment) 5714–1954, *Laws of the State of Israel,* Vol. 8 (5714–1953/54), p. 144.

16. See Shabtai Rosenne, "The Israel Nationality Law 5712–1952 and the Law of Return 5710–1950," *Journal du Droit International,* Vol. 81, No. 1 (January-February-March, 1954), pp. 4–63; Zvi Terlo, "The Immigration Laws of Israel—Some Problems," *Public Administration in Israel and Abroad 1965* (Jerusalem: Israel Institute of Public Administration, 1966), Vol. 6, pp. 31–51; Yehoshua Freudenheim, *Government in Israel* (Dobbs Ferry, N. Y.: Oceana Publications, Inc., 1967), pp. 253–62; M. D. Gouldman, *Israel Nationality Law* (Jerusalem: Hebrew University of Jerusalem, Faculty of Law, Institute for Legislative Research and Comparative Law, 1970), 151 pp., at 21–32; and Israel T. Naamani, *Israel: A Profile* (New York: Praeger Publishers, 1972), pp. 66–68.

17. Nationality Law 5712–1952, *Laws of the State of Israel,* Vol. 6 (5712–1951/52), pp. 50–53, as amended by Nationality (Amendment) Law 5718–1958, *Laws of the State of Israel,* Vol. 12 (5718–1957/58), p. 99. See also M. D. Gouldman, "Recent Changes in Israel's Nationality Law," *Israel Law Review* Vol. 4, No. 4 (October, 1969), pp. 551–58.

18. Sec. 1, Law of Return (Amendment No. 2) Law 5730–1970, *Laws of the State of Israel,* Vol. 24 (5730–1969/70), pp. 28–29. This section became Sec. 4B of the Law of Return.

MARRIAGE AND DIVORCE

19. Rabbinical Courts Jurisdiction (Marriage and Divorce) Law 5713–1953, *Laws of the State of Israel,* Vol. 7 (5713–1952/53), pp. 139–40; and Matters of Dissolution of Marriage (Jurisdiction in Special Cases) Law 5729–1969, *Laws of the State of Israel,* Vol. 23 (5729–1968/69), pp. 274–75. See also M. Chigier, "The Rabbinical Courts in the State of Israel," *Israel Law Review,* Vol. 2, No. 2 (April, 1967), pp. 147–81; Isaac S. Shiloh, "Marriage and Divorce in Israel," *Israel Law Review,* Vol. 5, No. 4

(October, 1970), pp. 479–98; and Joseph Laufer, "Israel's Supreme Court: The First Decade," *Journal of Legal Education,* Vol. 17, No. 1 (1964), pp. 43–62, at 57–58.

20. See Aharon M. K. Rabinowicz, "Human Rights in Israel," *Howard Law Journal,* Vol. II, No. 2 (Spring, 1965), pp. 300–15, at 303; Ariel Hecht, "Recent Developments Concerning Jurisdiction in Matters of Personal Status," *Israel Law Review,* Vol. 2, No. 4 (October, 1967), pp. 488–98; and Izhak Englard, "The Problem of Jewish Law in A Jewish State," *Israel Law Review,* Vol. 3, No. 2 (April, 1968), pp. 254–78.

21. Robert Gordis, "An American Conservative Rabbi Speaks," in Ruth Routtenberg Seldin and Carl Golden, *The Jewish State and the Jewish Religion* (New York: American Association for Jewish Education, 1973), p. 21.

22. Leviticus, 21:7.

23. For an Orthodox religious presentation of this point, see Getsel Ellinson, "Civil Marriage in Israel: Halakhic and Social Implications," *Tradition,* Vol. 13, No. 2 (Fall, 1972), pp. 24–34.

24. The bill would not authorize civil marriage for persons forbidden to marry because of blood relationship as defined by Orthodox rabbinical law. See *Israel Digest,* Vol. XV, No. 14 (July 7, 1972), p. 2. See also the section on the *Langer* case for a discussion of the question of "mamzerim." Chalitza is a Jewish religious ceremony which releases a male from the biblical obligation of marrying the widow of his childless brother. Such marriage, known as "Levirate marriage," has disappeared but the release ceremony is still an accepted Orthodox religious custom.

25. *Israel Digest,* Vol. XV, No. 7 (March 31, 1972), p. 2.

26. *Cohen and Bouslik v. Attorney General,* (1954) (I) 8 *Piskei Din* 4, and *Ganor v. Attorney General,* (1954) (I) 8 *Piskei Din* 833.

27. *Gurfinkel and Haklai v. Minister of the Interior,* (1963) (III) 17 *Piskei Din* 2048.

28. *Segev and Reichert v. Rabbinical Court of Safed,* (1967) (II) 21 *Piskei Din* 505. In all cases involving the private marriage loophole arrangement in which the Supreme Court has recognized the validity of the marriages, the marriage partners were Jews. In a recent case of a private marriage performed in Israel between an Israeli Jewish male and a Swiss Christian female, avowed atheists who rejected conversion and a religious ceremony, the Supreme Court refused to validate the marriage since it could not take effect at all under Jewish rabbinical law. Had the couple been married abroad, their marriage would have been considered valid insofar as the Supreme Court and Knesset are concerned. (*Tepper v. State of Israel,* (1974) (II) 28 *Piskei Din* 7)

29. *Rodnitzi v. The Rabbinical Court of Appeals,* (1970) (I) 24 *Piskei Din* 704.

30. *Jerusalem Post,* July 11, 1972, p. 1, and July 18, 1972, p. 5.

31. *Jewish Press,* July 14, 1972, p. 21. See also *Israel Digest,* Vol. XV, No. 14 (July 7, 1972), p. 3, and *Jerusalem Post,* July 18, 1972, p. 8. Acknowledging the need to prevent assimilation of Jews by mixed marriages, Premier Meir remarked: "I have often said, and will no doubt continue to say, that I oppose civil marriage. But I—and all religious people who do not blind themselves to reality—want to see solutions coming from the rabbis and spiritual leaders themselves." *Jerusalem Post,* July 18, 1972, p. 5.

32. *Israel Digest,* Vol. XV, No. 14 (July 7, 1972), p. 2.

33. *Israel Digest,* Vol. XV, No. 15 (July 21, 1972), p. 2.

34. *Israel Digest,* Vol. XV, No. 25 (December 8, 1972), p. 2. See Aaron Zwergbaum, "The Civil Marriage Controversy in Israel," *Congress bi-Weekly,* Vol. 30, No. 15 (November 4, 1963), pp. 18–20.

DIRECTIVES OF JANUARY 3, 1960

35. *New York Times,* January 4, 1960, p. 3.

LANDMARK CASES AND INCIDENTS, 1962–1969

Brother Daniel Case, 1962

36. *Oswald Rufeisen v. Minister of the Interior,* High Court 72/62, (1962) 16 *Piskei Din* (Law Reports) 2428. The case in English is contained in *Selected Judgments of the Supreme Court of Israel,* Special Volume, edited by Asher Felix Landau and Peter Elman (Jerusalem: The Ministry of Justice, 1971), 191 pp., at 1–34.

37. *New York Times,* March 15, 1962, p. 7, and November 20, 1962, p. 20.

38. *Time,* December 7, 1962, p. 54. See also *Time,* December 21, 1962, p. 11.

39. *New York Times,* December 7, 1962, p. 15.

40. *New York Times,* August 17, 1963, p. 22.

41. *Oswald Rufeisen v. Minister of the Interior, op. cit.,* 2443. See also *Selected Judgments of the Supreme Court of Israel, supra,* pp. 10–12, and

New York Times, December 7, 1962, p. 15, and *Israel Digest,* Vol. V, No. 26 (December 21, 1962), pp. 4–5.

42. *Selected Judgments of the Supreme Court of Israel, supra,* p. 13.

43. *Ibid.,* pp. 11–12.

44. *Ibid.,* p. 19.

45. *Ibid.,* p. 17.

46. In *Basan v. Basan,* (1965) 47 *Psakim Mehozi'im* (Judgments of the District Court) 417, the petitioner maintained that he had converted to Christianity in order to save his life but that he later re-identified with his Jewish religious origin—which Brother Daniel had not done.

47. Justice Silberg stated in the Court's decision: "According to the prevailing opinion in Jewish law, so it seems to me, a Jew who is converted or becomes an apostate continues to be treated as a Jew for all purposes save perhaps as to certain 'marginal' laws which have no real importance with regard to the central problem." (*Oswald Rufeisen v. Minister of the Interior, op. cit.,* 2432, and *Selected Judgments of the Supreme Court of Israel, supra,* p. 3.

48. For discussions of the *Brother Daniel* case see Solomon S. Bernards, *Who Is A Jew? A Reader* (New York: Anti-Defamation League of B'nai B'rith, no date), pp. 17–22; Max Lerner, "Who Is A Jew?," *New York Post,* December 7, 1962, p. 57; Yehuda Savir, "The Definition of A Jew Under Israel's Law of Return," *Southwestern Law Journal,* Vol. 17, No. 1 (March, 1963), pp. 123–33; "The Oswald Rufeisen (Brother Daniel) Case," *Midstream,* Vol. IX, No. 1 (March, 1963), pp. 78–96; Marc Galanter, "A Dissent on Brother Daniel," *Commentary,* Vol. 36, No. 1 (July 1963), pp. 10–17; Norman Bentwich, "Jewish Ethics in the Law and Courts of Israel," *Public Administration in Israel and Abroad 1964* (Jerusalem: Israel Institute of Public Administration, 1965), Vol. 5, pp. 18–22, at 21–22; R. Lehmann, "Nationality and Religion in Israel: Observations on the Rufeisen Case (Father Daniel)," *Journal du Droit International,* Vol. 90, No. 3 (July-August-September, 1963), pp. 694–717; Jack Segal, "Is An Apostate A Jew?," *Reconstructionist,* Vol. XXIX, No. 18 (January 10, 1964), pp. 10–14; Rabinowicz, *op. cit.,* pp. 309–10; Robert Gordis, *Judaism in A Christian World* (New York: McGraw-Hill Book Co., 1966), pp. 76–79; S. N. Eisenstadt, *Israeli Society* (New York: Basic Books, Inc., 1967), pp. 314–16; Amnon Rubinstein, "Law and Religion in Israel," *Israel Law Review,* Vol. 2, No. 3 (July, 1967), pp. 380–414, at 413–14; Birnbaum, *op. cit.,* p. 276; Simon N. Herman, *Israelis and Jews: The Continuity of an Identity* (New York: Random House, 1970), pp. 91–92; Norman L. Zucker, *The Coming Crisis in Israel: Private Faith and Public Policy* (Cambridge: Massachusetts Institute of Technology Press, 1973), pp. 179–88; and

Gideon Hausner, "The Rights of the Individual in Court," *Israel Law Review,* Vol. 9, No. 4 (October, 1974), pp. 486–88.

Funk-Schlesinger Case, 1963

49. *Henriette Anna Caterina Funk-Schlesinger v. Minister of the Interior,* High Court 143/62, (1963) 17 *Piskei Din* 225.

50. *Israel Digest,* Vol. VI, No. 5 (March 1, 1963), p. 8.

Matter of the Black Jews from India, 1961–65

51. *New York Times,* February 25, 1962, p. 28.

52. *Loc. cit.*

53. *Israel Digest,* Vol. VII, No. 17 (August 14, 1964), p. 6. Bitterness reached such intensity that an effigy of the Chief Rabbi with a rope around his neck was ceremoniously burned.

54. *New York Times,* August 18, 1964, p. 23. For excerpts of the Cabinet statement and Knesset resolution see *Israel Digest,* Vol. VII, No. 18 (August 28, 1964), p. 5.

55. The words "Bene Israel Community" in the February, 1962 directives were deleted and were replaced by the phrase "anyone concerning the ritual purity of whose family status any suspicion or doubt arises." *Israel Digest,* Vol. VII, No. 19 (September 11, 1964), p. 8. For a background of the Black Jews from India see Malka Hillel Shulewitz, "The B'nei Israel versus the Rabbinate," *Jewish Frontier,* Vol. XXX, No. 8 (October 1963), pp. 7–11; Ida G. Cowen, "Bene Israel and M'Dinat Israel," *Reconstructionist,* Vol. 30, No. 5 (April 17, 1964), pp. 12–20; Eisenstadt, *op. cit.,* pp. 312–14; Raphael Patai, *Tents of Jacob: The Diaspora—Yesterday and Today* (Englewood Cliffs, N.J.: Prentice-Hall, Inc., 1971), pp. 415–23; Schifra Strizower, *The Bene Israel of Bombay: A Study of a Jewish Community* (New York: Schocken Books, 1971); Douglas L. Greener, "The Three Jewries of India," *Israel Digest,* Vol. XVII, No. 26 (December 20, 1974), p. 4; and Gilbert Kushner, *Immigrants from India in Israel: Planned Change in an Administered Community* (Tucson: University of Arizona Press, 1973).

Ilana Stern Case, 1965

56. *Ilana Stern v. Minister of the Interior,* Jerusalem District Court, File 419/64 (June 23, 1965).

Rina Eitani Matter, 1965

57. See Jacob M. Chinitz, "Separation of State and Religion," *Jewish Spectator,* Vol. 39, No. 4 (Winter 1974), pp. 42–44.

58. See I. M. Lask, "When Is A Jew Not A Jew?," *American Zionist,* Vol. LV, No. 6 (March-April, 1965), pp. 13–14; Birnbaum, *op. cit.,* pp. 272–73; and Zucker, *op. cit.,* pp. 188–90.

59. S. Z. Abramov, "The Danger of a Religious Split in Jewry," *Midstream,* Vol. XII, No. 8 (October, 1966), pp. 3–13, at 13.

60. *National Jewish Monthly,* December, 1965, p. 10.

Problem of the Supreme Court Justice, 1966

61. *New York Times,* July 25, 1963, p. 3.

62. *New York Times,* March 24, 1966, p. 24.

63. *New York Times,* May 11, 1966, p. 10.

64. *Cohen and Bousslik v. Attorney General, op. cit.,* 239.

65. *Ganor v. Attorney General, op. cit.* See Laufer, "Israel's Supreme Court: The First Decade," *op. cit.,* pp. 57–58.

Falasha Wedding Case, 1968

66. *Gitiye v. The Chief Rabbinate and the Jerusalem Religious Council,* (1968) (I) 22 *Piskei Din* 290.

67. The term "Falasha" in Amharic signifies "exiles," "strangers" or "immigrants." It is a term used by Christians and Moslems for members of a group of tribes of black Ethiopians, numbering about 20,000 of whom 350 have settled in Israel, who call themselves "House of Israel" ("Beit Israel") and practice a religion closely resembling Judaism insofar as the laws of Moses and the Old Testament are concerned. They observe the Mosaic biblical laws on food, circumcision and purification, but do not acknowledge or accept the Talmud which together with the Old Testament forms the basis of traditional, Orthodox Judaism. It is generally held that they descend from converts who adopted Judaism prior to the Christian era, although one Falasha legend in Ethiopia holds them to be direct descendants of Manelik I, the son of the Queen of Sheba and King Solomon of Israel. Others suggest that the first Falashas were the offspring of Yemenite Jewish traders who settled in the ancient Ethiopian kingdom of Axum but were later forced to hide when the country was converted to Coptic Christianity in the Fourth Century C. E. The Falashas in Israel maintain that they are the direct descendants of the ancient Israelite tribe

of Dan and are linked in ancestry to Moses when he was King of Ethiopia in 1313 B.C.E. after leading an Egyptian army which conquered Ethiopia. See Israel Goldstein, "Falashas: Ethiopia's Jews," *National Jewish Monthly,* December, 1969, pp. 14–17; Arnold Sherman, "Today's Falashas," *Israel Magazine,* Vol. IV, No. 9 (September, 1972), pp. 45–53; Patai, *Tents of Jacob, op. cit.,* pp. 423–26; and Erika Oyserman, "Meet the Falashas," *Israel Digest,* Vol. XVII, No. 14 (July 5, 1974), p. 7.

68. *Bassan v. Supreme Rabbinical Appeal Court,* (1964) (IV) 18 *Piskei Din* 309.

69. M. D. Gouldman, "The Falasha Wedding," *Israel Law Review,* Vol. 3, No. 4 (October, 1968), pp. 595–99, at 599. See also Birnbaum, *op. cit.,* p. 272.

70. Oyserman, *op. cit.,* p. 7.

71. *Jewish Press,* August 23, 1974, p. 16. A plea for Israel to deem the Falashas in Ethiopia as Jews and bring them all to Israel was made by Graenum Berger, "An Open Letter to the Labor Zionist Movement About the Ethiopian Jews (Falashas)," *Jewish Frontier,* Vol. XLI, No. 7 (September, 1974), pp. 14–19.

72. *Jewish Floridian,* November 1, 1974, p. 11-A. In April, 1975 an inter-ministerial committee of experts, created to examine into the "Jewishness" of the Falashas and headed by the Ministry of Justice's Director General, Zvi Terlo, determined that the Falashas are full-fledged Jews and must be recognized as eligible for Israeli citizenship and other rights under the Law of Return. However, the Ashkenazi Chief Rabbi, Shlomo Goren, at once condemned the decision, insisting that only a body of Orthodox experts on rabbinical law ("halachah") could decide such issues. The Sephardic Chief Rabbi, Ovadia Yosef, who has long maintained that the Falashas are full-fledged Jews and who advised the inter-ministerial committee on rabbinical law, disagreed with Rabbi Goren and further pointed out that it is the duty of Israeli Jewry to save the Ethiopian Falashas from oppression and possible destruction by encouraging their immigration to Israel and facilitating their entry into the Jewish community. ("Falasha Jews Immigrate," *Israel Digest,* Vol. XVIII, No. 9 (April 25, 1975), pp. 6–7) Shortly afterwards, the Minister of Religious Affairs, Yitzhak Raphael, appeared to have second thoughts, expressed uncertainty about the inter-ministerial committee's decision, and urged that the matter be referred to the Cabinet for final decision. (*Jerusalem Post,* Weekly Overseas Edition, April 29, 1975, p. 4) See also Louis Rapoport, "The Falashas: Next Year in Jerusalem," *Jeruslaem Post Magazine,* April 12, 1974, pp. 14–16; Meyer Levin, "The Last of the Falashas?," *Midstream,* Vol. XXI, No. 6 (June/July,

1975), pp. 44–49; Haim Schachter, "Falashas—Old–New Jews," *Jewish Digest*, Vol. XXI, No. 1 (October 1975), pp. 54–56; and *New York Times*, November 2, 1975, p. 27.

Matter of the Marranos, 1966–1970

73. "Chuetas," like the word "Marrano," is also a Spanish term meaning swine. In Hebrew the word describing such people is "Anussim" which means "those compelled"; and the Arabic term for them is "Murain" denoting hypocrites.

74. *New York Times*, October 3, 1966, p. 13.

75. Joseph B. Schechtman, "Marranos in Israel," *American Zionist* (April, 1967), pp. 15–16.

76. *Israel Digest*, Vol. XIII, No. 23 (November 13, 1970), p. 8.

Shalit Case, 1969

77. *Benjamin Shalit (in his name and for his children) v. Minister of the Interior and Registration Clerk, Haifa*, High Court 58/68, (1969)(II) 23 *Piskei Din* 477. For the text of the decision in English see Landau and Elman (editors), *Selected Judgments of the Supreme Court of Israel, supra* note 36, pp. 35–191.

78. *New York Times*, October 18, 1968, p. 5.

79. Population Registry Law, 5725–1965, Vol. 19, *Laws of the State of Israel* (5725–1964/65), p. 288.

80. *Shalit v. Minister of Interior, op. cit.*, p. 505.

81. *Ibid.*, p. 477.

82. *Ibid.*, p. 489.

83. *New York Times*, January 21, 1972, p. 14.

84. Benjamin Akzin, "Who Is A Jew? A Hard Case," *Israel Law Review*, Vol. 5, No. 2 (April, 1970), pp. 259–63, at 263. See also Herman, *op. cit.*, pp. 95–96; Birnbaum, *op. cit.*, p. 276; Zvi Ben-Moshe, "Reactions to the Shalit Case," *Congress bi-Weekly*, Vol. 37, No. 4 (March 6, 1970), pp. 4–5; Robert Alter, "The Shalit Case," *Commentary*, Vol. 50, No. 1 (July, 1970), pp. 55–61; and Zucker, *op. cit.*, pp. 190–201.

85. *New York Times*, January 24, 1970, p. 6. See also Doris Lankin, "High Court makes procedural ruling in 'Who is a Jew?' case," *Jerusalem Post*, January 25, 1970, pp. 4–5.

1970 AMENDMENT TO THE LAW OF RETURN

86. Law of Return (Amendment No. 2) Law, 5730–1970, *op. cit.*, pp. 28–29.

87. *New York Times,* January 26, 1970, p. 1.

88. *New York Times,* January 30, 1970, p. 1.

89. *New York Times,* February 2, 1970, p. 6.

90. *New York Times,* February 4, 1970, p. 4.

91. *New York Times,* March 11, 1970, p. 3.

92. Sec. 1, Law of Return (Amendment No. 2) Law, *op. cit.*, p. 28, which added a Sec. 4B to the Law of Return; and Sec. 3A (b), Population Registry Law, 5725–1965, *Laws of the State of Israel,* Vol. 19 (5725–1964/65), pp. 288–97. See also *Israel Digest,* Vol. XIII, No. 4 (20 February 1970), p. 4. At first the Cabinet, threatened with resignation from the Coalition by the National Religious Party unless the Knesset by legislation reversed the Supreme Court's decision in the *Shalit* case, gave in and made such a recommendation to the Knesset. Public opinion, however, forced the Cabinet to withdraw the recommendation, and then the Cabinet drew up the compromise proposal.

93. In June, 1970 Mrs. Helen Zeidman converted to Judaism in the United States under the Reform procedure, settled in Israel as an immigrant, and was denied registration as a Jew. She applied to the Supreme Court but then underwent Orthodox conversion to Judaism before the Court could render judgment. See the section on the "Helen Zeidman Matter, 1970" for details.

94. Law of Return (Amendment No. 2) Law, *op. cit.*, p. 28. See also Misha Louvish, "Who is a Jew?," *Israel Digest,* Vol. XV, No. 15 (July 21, 1972), p. 4.

95. Sec. 3A, Population Registry Law, 5725–1965, *op. cit.*, p. 288.

96. In the Proclamation of Independence of 1948 and in a number of law the term "Jew" was mentioned but no attempt to define who is a Jew was made until the March 10, 1970 legislation following the Supreme Court decision in the *Shalit* case. Administratively, however, the Ministry of the Interior, in its directives guiding the registration clerks, defined who is a Jew for purposes of maintaining the Population Register and of certifying entries on the identity cards. The portfolio of Minister of the Interior has been held by the National Religious Party.

97. Shalev Ginossar, "Who Is A Jew: A Better Law?", *Israel Law Review,* Vol. 5, No. 2 (April, 1970), pp. 264–67.

98. Misha Louvish, "The 'Who Is a Jew?' Question," *Israel Digest,* Vol. XVII, No. 3 (February 1, 1974), p. 3.

LANDMARK CASES AND INCIDENTS, 1970–1973

Helen Zeidman Matter, 1970

99. Whether the 1970 Amendment to the Law of Return intended to include converts to Judaism under all practices rather than solely under the Orthodox practice is unclear. However, on the second reading of the amendment bill in the Knesset a proposal to substitute "converted to Judaism in accordance with the Halacha" for "converted to Judaism" was defeated. *Divrei Ha'Knesset* (Proceedings of the Knesset), Vol. 56 (1970), pp. 1137, 1143 and 1170.

100. *New York Times,* June 16, 1970, p. 13, and June 17, 1970, p. 11. Although Orthodox conversion procedure usually takes a year or more, Rabbi Shlomo Goren, former Chief Chaplain of the Israeli army and then a candidate for Chief Rabbi of the Ashkenazi Jews in Israel, anxious to prevent the probable ruling in favor of Mrs. Zeidman, found a basis for converting her according to Orthodox practice before a rabbinical court consisting of himself and two army chaplains just hours before the Supreme Court was to meet to render its decision. (*New York Times,* March 7, 1972, p. 8)

I. Ben Menashe Case, 1970

101. *Menashe v. Minister of the Interior,* (1970) (I) 24 *Piskei Din* 105.
102. See *Israel Law Review,* Vol. 9, No. 1 (January, 1974), p. 146.

Rodnitzi Case and the Religious Ban on "Cohens" Marrying Divorcees, 1970

103. *Elkana Rodnitzi v. The Rabbinical Court of Appeals,* High Court of Justice, 51/69, (1970) (I) 24 *Piskei Din* 704.
104. *Gurfinkel and Haklai v. Minister of the Interior,* (1963) (III) 17 *Piskei Din* 2048.
105. *New York Times,* June 17, 1970, p. 11.

Zigi Staderman Case, 1970

106. *Staderman v. Minister of the Interior,* (1970) (I) 24 *Piskei Din* 766.
107. Population Registry Law, 5725–1965, *op. cit.,* pp. 288–97.
108. See M. D. Gouldman's comments on this case in the *Israel Law Review,* Vol. 6, No. 3 (July, 1971), pp. 427–28.

Matter of the Karaites, 1961–1971

109. Case 1293/5726, cited in the *Israel Law Review,* Vol. 6, No. 4 (October, 1971), p. 595.

110. *Jewish Press,* March 23, 1973, p. 8. The Karaites are not only considered by the Orthodox rabbinate in Israel to be less than full-fledged Jews, but they are also not permitted to form a separate religious community with their own religious leadership and courts, as are the Jewish, Moslem, Christian, and Druze religious communities.

Yolanda Gerstel Matter, 1971

111. *Israel Magazine,* Vol. IV, No. 1 (January, 1972), p. 4.

112. *Jewish Press,* July 14, 1972, p. 17.

George Raphael Tamarin Case, 1972

113. *George Raphael Tamarin v. State of Israel,* (1972) (I) 26 *Piskei Din* 197. See also Naamani, *Israel: A Profile, op. cit.,* p. 69.

114. *New York Times,* January 21, 1972, p. 14.

115. *Israel Digest,* Vol. XV, No. 4 (February 18, 1972), p. 3.

116. For a critical opinion of this point see Nissim Rejwan, "Discord in Israel," *Dissent,* Vol. XIX (Spring, 1972), pp. 318–21.

Otto Preminger-Hope Price Matter, 1972

117. See Willi Frischauer, *Behind the Scenes of Otto Preminger* (New York: William Morrow & Co., 1974), pp. 188–89.

118. *New York Times,* November 18, 1972, p. 29.

Langer Case, 1972

119. *The Judgment in the Matter of the Brother and the Sister,* Supreme Rabbinical Court of Jerusalem, Chief Rabbi Shlomo Goren, President (Jerusalem: Government Press, Tevet, 5733), 200 pp. (in Hebrew only).

120. Talmud, Third Order, "Nashim": First Tractate, Chapters 2, 4, 5 and 6; and Fifth Tractate, Chapter 9. See also R. J. Zwi Werblowsky and Geoffrey Wigoder (ed.), *The Encyclopedia of the Jewish Religion* (New York: Holt, Rinehart and Winston, Inc., 1965), pp. 198, 248–49, and 250–52; and Hayyim Schneid (ed.), "Prohibited Marriages," in *Marriage* (Philadelphia: Jewish Publication Society of America, 1973, pp. 79–95. In Or-

thodox religious law there are marriages which are forbidden and the offspring of which will be deemed "mamzerim." Such prohibited marriages are not limited to cases of cosanguinity—blood relationship—but include also cases of affinity—relationship through marriage. Cases of cosanguinity are: between a man and his mother, sister, daughter, granddaughter, father's sister, or mother's sister. Cases of affinity are: between a man and his stepmother; between father-in-law and daughter-in-law; between mother-in-law and son-in-law; between a widower or divorced man and the daughter or granddaughter of the wife; between brother-in-law and sister-in-law; and between a man and his uncle's wife. In these primary cases of forbidden marriages no religious divorce ("geht") is possible or required, and the offspring of such marriages are deemed "mamzerim." There is, also, a secondary class of prohibited marriages which, if contracted, must be dissolved by an Orthodox religious divorce, but the children born of such marriages are not considered "mamzerim." These are: between a man and his grandmother or great-grandmother; between a man and his grandfather's later wife; and between a man and the wife of his dead or divorced grandson. In addition there is a special kind of marriage that is biblically banned: between a man who is a "Cohen"—a member of the priestly class descending from Aaron, the high priest brother of Moses—and a divorcee. If such a marriage is contracted, no religious divorce is possible or required, and the children of the marriage are deemed "mamzerim."

Interestingly, while a "mamzer" is not considered a full-fledged Jew under Orthodox religious law, he or she inherits from the father equally with legitimate offspring.

121. *New York Times,* November 20, 1972, p. 5; *Israel Digest,* Vol. XV, No. 25 (December 8, 1972), p. 2; and *Jerusalem Post,* November 20, 1972, p. 1.

122. *New York Post,* November 20, 1972, p. 26.

123. *New York Times,* November 30, 1972, p. 87.

124. *Jewish Press,* February 16, 1973, p. 8.

125. *Israel Digest,* Vol. XVI, No. 8 (April 13, 1973), p. 8.

126. *Jewish Press,* January 12, 1973, pp. 16 and 44. See Zucker, *op. cit.,* p. 245.

127. *Jewish Press,* December 15, 1972, p. 45.

Yeshayahu Shik Case, 1973

128. *Shik v. Attorney General,* (1973) (II) 27 *Piskei Din* 3.

129. As amended, the Population Registry Law now provides that "a

person shall not be registered as a Jew by nationality ["le'um" meaning ethnic affiliation] or religion if a notification under this Law . . . or a public document indicates that he is not a Jew." The application here is to change an initial registration or to change an existing registration made without the person's knowledge or consent.

130. For a brief explanation of the case, see *Israel Law Review,* Vol. 9, No. 1 (January, 1974), pp. 146–47, and Vol. 10, No. 1 (January 1975), pp. 131–32.

Case of the American Black Israelites, 1969–1973

131. *Clark v. Minister of the Interior,* (1973) (I) 27 *Piskei Din* 113.
132. *New York Times,* December 23, 1969, p. 9.
133. *New York Times,* August 31, 1971, p. 3.
134. *Loc. cit.*
135. *New York Times,* October 8, 1971, p. 2.
136. *New York Times,* December 20, 1971, p. 4.
137. *New York Post,* January 24, 1972, p. 37.
138. *New York Times,* September 5, 1973, p. 2.
139. *New York Times,* October 5, 1973, p. 11.
140. *Clark v. Minister of the Interior, op. cit.* See also *New York Times,* October 4, 1973, p. 5. In a recent, penetrating article, J. David Bleich, an American Orthodox rabbi, asserted: "With the exception of the Falashas, whose claim to Jewish identity was, according to rabbinic sources, predicated upon a claim to descent from the tribe of Dan and who, in any event, are not known to have been of definite gentile genealogical origin, all contemporary Black Jews are known to have been *bechezket akum,* i.e., to have been descended from progenitors known to have conducted and identified themselves as non-Jews. . . . When no claim to prior conversion is made—and indeed many find the very suggestion insulting since they contend that they, and they alone, are descendants of the original Jewish people—any claim to Jewish identity on their part must be rejected as spurious." (J. David Bleich, "Black Jews: A Halakhic Perspective," *Tradition,* Vol. 15, Nos. 1 and 2 (Spring-Summer, 1975), pp. 59–60) See also Robert G. Weisbord, "Israel and the Black Hebrew Israelites," *Judaism,* Vol. 24, No. 1 (Winter, 1975), pp. 23–38.

PROPOSED AMENDMENTS TO THE LAW OF RETURN,
1972–1974

141. *Jerusalem Post,* July 4, 1972, pp. 1–2, and *New York Post,* July 3, 1972, p. 4.

142. *Jerusalem Post,* July 11, 1972, p. 1. The National Religious Party then held eleven seats in the Knesset and three portfolios in the Cabinet. A Deputy Minister of Education, Dr. Avner Sciaky, was dismissed from his position for violating collective Cabinet responsibility by voting in the Knesset for the two bills instead of abstaining or voting against them. (*Jerusalem Post,* July 18, 1972, p. 1) Further complicating the problem, the two Chief Rabbis of Israel took opposing stands. One, Yehuda Unterman of the Ashkenazi community, urged all Orthodox Knesset Members to support the two bills, whereas Yitzhak Nissim of the Sephardic community permitted abstention. (*Ibid.,* p. 5)

143. *New York Times,* July 13, 1972, p. 9, and *New York Post,* July 13, 1972, p. 53.

144. *Jerusalem Post,* July 18, 1972, p. 5.

145. *Loc. cit.*

146. *Times of Israel and World Jewish Review,* Vol. 1, No. 6 (May 1974), p. 80.

147. *Jerusalem Post Weekly* (Weekly Overseas Edition), April 9, 1974, p. 7.

148. High Court of Justice 87/74.

149. *New York Times,* March 21, 1974, p. 10.

150. See Naomi Shepherd, "Israelis in Search of Themselves," *New York Times,* July 21, 1974, p. 16E.

151. *Israel Digest,* Vol. XVII, No. 23 (November 8, 1974), p. 8. The religious issue of conversion was not the only point of difference in this bitter struggle. The National Religious Party was opposed also to the relinquishing by Israel of any part of the ancestral, biblical territory on the West Bank of the Jordan River; and it promised that it would vote in the Cabinet and Knesset against any such relinquishment. Premier Rabin agreed to call new parliamentary elections before signing a treaty involving the surrender of any such territory. (*New York Times,* October 25, 1974, p. 4)

CONCLUSION: Is There a Solution?

152. *New York Times,* April 4, 1971, p. 16. See also *Israel Digest,* Vol. XIV, No. 13 (June 25, 1971), p. 6.

153. See Victor Solomon, *A Handbook on Conversions to the Religions of the World* (Stravon Educational Press, 1965), pp. 32–67, for a description of the conversion processes under the Orthodox, Conservative and Reform Jewish communities. See also Philip Birnbaum, *A Book of Jewish Concepts* (New York: Hebrew Publishing Co., 1964), pp. 132–34; and Theodore Friedman, "Conversion and Conservative Judaism," *Conservative Judaism,* Vol. XXVIII, No. 3 (Spring 1974), pp. 21–29.

154. Talmud, *Shakh on Yoreh Deah,* 267.8.

155. Old Testament, II *Kings* 17.25.

156. Talmud, *Gerim,* 1.3.

157. J. J. Goldberg, "Who Is A Jew?," *Jewish Frontier,* Vol. XLI, No. 3 (March 1974), pp. 44–47.

158. For a critical comment on the Orthodox rabbinate's stand on conversions and its effect on Jewry outside of Israel, see "Conversion and Jewish Law," *Jewish Spectator,* Vol. 39, No. 3 (Fall 1974), pp. 5–7. For a brief discussion of the linkage of "Who Is A Convert?" to "Who Is A Jew?," see Zvi Soifer, "Who Is A Jew?," *Israel Digest,* Vol. XVII, No. 21 (October 11, 1974), p. 7.

159. *The Southern Company and Marbek Ltd. v. The Chief Rabbinical Council,* (1964) (II) 18 *Piskei Din* 324.

160. See Sholom J. Kahn, "Israeli, Hebrew, Jew: The Semantic Problem," *Judaism,* Vol. 19, No. 1 (Winter 1970), pp. 9–13.

161. Haim Cohen, Justice of the Supreme Court of Israel, recently has been publicly urging the Conservative and Reform rabbis to challenge in Israel's courts the Orthodox rabbinate's exclusive authority over the marriage, divorce and conversion of Jews in Israel, and he has predicted the success of such a challenge. A more desirable method, which would not result in open, bitter conflict, is agreement among the three rabbinates.

162. The bitterness of the *Langer* case decision has not entirely dissipated. In July, 1975 Rabbi Shlomo Lorincz, a Member of the Knesset from the ultra-Orthodox Agudat Israel Party who vehemently opposed Chief Rabbi Shlomo Goren's ruling in the *Langer* case, rose in the Knesset and accused Rabbi Goren of dictatorial, tyrannical and vengeful practices similar to those of President Idi Amin of Uganda for selecting the candidates for rabbinical judgeships from among his supporters and blocking those who did not support him. Angered by the denunciation, Rabbi Goren convened the Chief Rabbinical Council which he heads, and the

Council excommunicated Rabbi Lorincz. (Israeli rabbis divided over cherem edict," *Jewish Chronicle,* August 8, 1975, p. 2). (*New York Times,* August 1, 1975, p. 4) A large section of the ultra-Orthodox rabbinical elements have rallied behind Rabbi Lorincz. ("Israeli rabbis divided over cherem edict," *Jewish Chronicle,* August 8, 1975, p. 2) Also, the feud between Sephardic Chief Rabbi Ovadia Yosef and Rabbi Goren has expanded and there is almost total discord between the two. See Stephen Oren, "Who Is a Jew—Round III," *Midstream,* Vol. XXI, No. 6 (June/-July, 1975), pp. 38–44.

In September, 1975 it was revealed that a "Marriage Disabilities List" is maintained by the Ministry of Religious Affairs of about 2,200 Jewish Israelis ineligible for marriage in Israel. While the list is considered legal by the Attorney General and the Cabinet, the disclosure resulted in talk of reviving Gideon Hausner's civil marriage bill. (*Jerusalem Post,* October 21, 1975, p. 3).

Bibliography

Books and Pamphlets

Bernards, Solomon S. *Who Is A Jew? A Reader.* New York. Anti-Defamation League of B'nai Brith. No date. 63 pp.

Birnbaum, Ervin. *The Politics of Compromise: State and Religion in Israel.* Rutherford, N.J. Fairleigh Dickinson University Press. 1970.

Birnbaum, Philip. *A Book of Jewish Concepts.* New York. Hebrew Publishing Co. 1964. Pp. 132–34.

Eisenstadt, S. N. *Israeli Society.* New York. Basic Books, Inc. 1967.

Freudenheim, Yehoshua. *Government in Israel.* Dobbs Ferry, N.Y. Oceana Publications, Inc. 1967. Pp. 253–62.

Frischauer, Willi. *Behind the Scenes of Otto Preminger.* New York. William Morrow & Co. 1974. Pp. 188–89.

Goldman, Eliezer. *Religious Issues in Israel's Political Life.* Jerusalem. Mador Dati, The Youth and he-Haluz Department of the World Zionist Organization. 1964.

Gordis, Robert. *Judaism in A Christian World.* New York. McGraw-Hill Book Co. 1966. Pp. 76–79.

Gouldman, M. D. *Israel Nationality Law.* Jerusalem. Hebrew University of Jerusalem, Faculty of Law, Institute for Legislative Research and Comparative Law. 1970.

Gruen, George E. *Again "Who Is A Jew?": Some Aspects of Religion and Law in Israel.* New York. American Jewish Committee. 1970. 12 pp.

Herman, Simon N. *Israelis and Jews: The Continuity of an Identity.* New York. Random House. 1970.

Hoenig, Sidney B. and Litvin, Baruch. *Jewish Identity: Modern Responsa and Opinions on The Registration of Children of Mixed Marriages.* New York. Philipp Feldheim, Inc. 1965.

Kushner, Gilbert. *Immigrants from India in Israel: Planned Change in an Administered Community.* Tucson. University of Arizona Press. 1973.

Landau, Asher Felix and Elman, Peter (editors). *Selected Judgments of the Supreme Court of Israel.* Special Volume. Jerusalem. The Ministry of Justice. 1971.

Naamani, Israel T. *Israel: A Profile.* New York. Praeger Publishers. 1972.

Patai, Raphael. *Tents of Jacob: The Diaspora—Yesterday and Today.* Englewood Cliffs, N.J. Prentice-Hall, Inc. 1971. Pp. 415–23.

Schneerson, Menachem M. *Who Is A Jew.* Brooklyn, N.Y. Vaad L'Hafotzas Sichos. Seventh Year Special Issue. Vol. VII, No. 9. September, 1974. 11 pp.

Schneid, Hayyim (ed.). *Marriage.* Philadelphia. Jewish Publication Society of America. 1973. Pp. 79–95.

Solomon, Victor. *A Handbook on Conversions to the Religions of the World.* Stravon Educational Press. 1965. Pp. 32–67.

Strizower, Schifra. *The Bene Israel of Bombay: A Study of a Jewish Community.* New York. Schocken Books. 1971.

Werblowsky, R. J. Zwi and Wigoder, Geoffrey (editors). *The Encyclopedia of the Jewish Religion.* New York. Holt, Rinehart and Winston, Inc. 1965.

Zucker, Norman L. *The Coming Crisis in Israel: Private Faith and Public Policy.* Cambridge. Massachusetts Institute of Technology Press. 1973.

Articles

Abramov, S. Z. "The Danger of a Religious Split in Jewry." *Midstream.* Vol. XII, No. 8. October, 1966. Pp. 3–13.

Akzin, Benjamin. "Who Is A Jew? A Hard Case." *Israel Law Review.* Vol. 5, No. 2. April, 1970. Pp. 259–63.

Alter, Robert. "The Shalit Case." *Commentary.* Vol. 50, No. 1. July, 1970. Pp. 55–61.

Baron, Salo W. "Who Is A Jew? Some Historical Reflections." *Midstream.* Vol. VI, No. 2. Spring, 1960. Pp. 5–16.

Ben-Moshe, Zvi. "Reactions to the Shalit Case." *Congress bi-Weekly.* Vol. 37, No. 4. March 6, 1970. Pp. 4–5.

Bentwich, Norman. "Jewish Ethics in the Law and Courts of Israel." *Public Administration in Israel and Abroad 1964.* Jerusalem. Israel Institute of Public Administration. 1965. Vol. 5. Pp. 18–22.

Berger, Graenum. "An Open Letter to the Labor Zionist Movement About the Ethiopian Jews (Falashas)." *Jewish Frontier.* Vol. XLI, No. 7. September, 1974. Pp. 14–19.

Bleich, J. David. "Black Jews: A Halakhic Perspective." *Tradition.* Vol. 15, Nos. 1 and 2. Spring-Summer, 1975. Pp. 48–79.

Chigier, M. "The Rabbinical Courts in the State of Israel." *Israel Law Review.* Vol. 2, No. 2. April, 1967. Pp. 147–81.

Chinitz, Jacob M. "Separation of State and Religion." *Jewish Spectator.* Vol. 39, No. 4. Winter 1974. Pp. 42–44.

Cohon, Samuel S. "Who is a Jew?" *Central Conference of American Rabbis Journal.* Issue No. 26. June, 1959. pp. 9–13.

"Conversion and Jewish Law." *Jewish Spectator.* Vol. 39, No. 3. Fall 1974. Pp. 5–7.

Cowen, Ida G. "Bene Israel and M'Dinat Israel." *Reconstructionist.* Vol. 30, No. 5. April 17, 1964. Pp. 12–20.

Ellinson, Getsel. "Civil Marriage in Israel: Halakhic and Social Implications." *Tradition.* Vol. 13, No. 2. Fall, 1972. Pp. 24–34.

England, Izhak. "The Problem of Jewish Law in A Jewish State." *Israel Law Review.* Vol. 3, No. 2. April, 1968. Pp. 254–78.

Friedman, Theodore. "Conversion and Conservative Judaism." *Conservative Judaism.* Vol. XXVIII, No. 3. Spring 1974. pp. 21–29.

Galanter, Marc. "A Dissent on Brother Daniel." *Commentary.* Vol. 36, No. 1. July 1963. Pp. 10–17.

Ginossar, Shalev. "Who Is A Jew: A Better Law?" *Israel Law Review.* Vol. 5, No. 2. April 1970. Pp. 264–67.

Goldberg, J. J. "Who Is A Jew?" *Jewish Frontier.* Vol. XLI, No. 3. March 1974. Pp. 44–47.

Goldstein, Israel. "Falashas: Ethiopia's Jews." *National Jewish Monthly.* December, 1969. Pp. 14–17.

Gordis, Robert. "An American Conservative Rabbi Speaks." In Selden, Ruth Routtenberg and Golden, Carl (editors). *The Jewish State and the Jewish Religion.* New York. American Association for Jewish Education. 1973. Pp. 20–21.

———. "Brother Daniel and His Brother Jews: The Paradox of the Decision." *Congress bi-Weekly.* Vol. 30, No. 3. February 4, 1963. Pp. 5–7.

———. "The Uniqueness of the Jewish People." *Congress bi-Weekly.* Vol. 30, No. 4. February 18, 1963. Pp. 9–11.

———. "The Status of the Jewish Convert." *Congress bi-Weekly.* Vol. 30, No. 5. March 4, 1963. Pp. 7–8.

Gouldman, M. D. "Recent Changes in Israel's Nationality Law." *Israel Law Review.* Vol. 4, No. 4. October, 1969. Pp. 551–58.

―――. "The Falasha Wedding." *Israel Law Review.* Vol. 3, No. 4. October, 1968. Pp. 595–99.

Greener, Douglas L. "The Three Jewries of India." *Israel Digest.* Vol. XVII, No. 26. December 20, 1974. P. 4.

Halpern, Ben. "Who is a Jew?" *Jewish Frontier.* Vol. XXVI, No. 1. January 1959. Pp. 7–10.

Hausner, Gideon. "The Rights of the Individual in Court." *Israel Law Review.* Vol. 9, No. 4. October, 1974. Pp. 486–88.

Hecht, Ariel. "Recent Developments Concerning Jurisdiction in Matters of Personal Status." *Israel Law Review.* Vol. 2, No. 4. October, 1967. Pp. 488–98.

Kahn, Sholom J. "Israeli, Hebrew, Jew: The Semantic Problem." *Judaism.* Vol. 19, No. 1. Winter 1970. Pp. 9–13.

Kallen, Horace M.; Berkovits, Eliezer; Olan, Levi A.; and Menes, Abraham. "Who is a Jew? A Symposium." *Judaism.* Vol. 8, 1. Winter, 1959. Pp. 3–15.

Kreitman, Benjamin Z.; Stern, Jack, Jr.; Gershfield, Edward; and Rozenberg, Martin. "Who Is A Jew: A Symposium." *Conservative Judaism.* Vol. XXIV, No. 4. Summer 1970. Pp. 21–35.

Lankin, Doris. "High Court makes procedural ruling in 'Who is a Jew?' case." *Jerusalem Post.* January 25, 1970. Pp. 4–5.

Lask, I. M. "When Is A Jew Not A Jew? *American Zionist.* Vol. LV, No. 6. March-April, 1965. Pp. 13–14.

Laufer, Joseph. "Israel's Supreme Court: The First Decade." *Journal of Legal Education.* Vol. 17, No. 1. 1964. Pp. 43–62.

Lehmann, R. "Nationality and Religion in Israel: Observations on the Rufeisen Case (Father Daniel)." *Journal du Droit International.* Vol. 90, No. 3. July-August-September, 1963. Pp. 694–717

Lerner, Max. "Who Is A Jew?" *New York Post.* December 7, 1962. P. 57.

Levin, Meyer. "The Last of the Falashas?" *Midstream.* Vol. XXI, No. 6. June/July, 1975. Pp. 44–49.

Levy, Richard N.; Wright, Norman; Maller, Allen S.; Agus, Robert; and Friedman, Richard. "The Convert." *Davka.* Vol. V, No. 1. Winter 1975. Pp. 4–25.

Loewe, Raphael. "Defining Judaism: Some Ground-Clearing." *Jewish Journal of Sociology.* Vol. VII, No. 2. December 1965. Pp. 153–75.

Lookstein, Joseph H. "Who Is A Jew? Question for Israel and World Jewry." *Jewish Press.* September 1, 1972. Pp. 25 and 33.

Louvish, Misha. "The 'Who Is a Jew?' Question." *Israel Digest.* Vol. XVII, No. 3. February 1, 1974. P. 3.

_____. "Who is a Jew?" *Israel Digest.* Vol. XV, No. 15. July 21, 1972. P. 4.

"The Oswald Rufeisen (Brother Daniel) Case. *Midstream.* Vol. IX, No. 1. March, 1963. Pp. 78–96.

Oren, Stephen. "Who Is a Jew—Round III." *Midstream.* Vol. XXI, No. 6. June/July, 1975. Pp. 38–44.

Oyserman, Erika. "Meet the Falashas." *Israel Digest.* Vol. XVII, No. 14. July 5, 1974. P. 7.

Petuchowsky, Jakob J. "Who is a Jew?" *Jewish Frontier.* Vol. XXVI, No. 6. June 1959. Pp. 6–10.

Rabinowicz, Aharon M. K. "Human Rights in Israel." *Howard Law Journal.* Vol. II, No. 2. Spring, 1965. Pp. 300–15.

Rapoport, Louis. "The Falashas: Next Year in Jerusalem." *Jerusalem Post Magazine.* April 12, 1974. Pp. 14–16.

Rejwan, Nissim. "Discord in Israel." *Dissent.* Vol. XIX. Spring, 1972. Pp. 318–21.

Rosenne, Shabtai. "The Israel Nationality Law 5712–1952 and the Law of Return 5710–1950." *Journal du Droit International.* Vol. 81, No. 1. January-February-March, 1954. Pp. 4–63.

Roshwald, Mordecai. "Marginal Gentiles in Israel." *Judaism.* Vol. 24, No. 1. Winter 1975. Pp. 23–38.

Rubinstein, Amnon. "Law and Religion in Israel." *Israel Law Review.* Vol. 2, No. 3. July, 1967. Pp. 380–414.

Savir, Yehuda. "The Definition of A Jew Under Israel's Law of Return." *Southwestern Law Journal.* Vol. 17, No. 1. March, 1963. Pp. 123–33.

Schachter, Haim. "Falashas—Old–New Jews." *Jewish Digest.* Vol. XXI, No. 1. October 1975. Pp. 54-56.

Schechtman, Joseph B. "Marranos in Israel." *American Zionist.* April, 1967. Pp. 15–16.

Segal, Jack. "Is An Apostate A Jew?" *Reconstructionist.* Vol. XXIX, No. 18. January 10, 1964. Pp. 10–14.

Shepherd, Naomi. "Israelis in Search of Themselves." *New York Times.* July 21, 1974. P. 16E.

Sherman, Arnold. "Today's Falashas." *Israel Magazine.* Vol. IV, No. 9. September, 1972. Pp. 45–53.

Shiloh, Isaac S. "Marriage and Divorce in Israel." *Israel Law Review.* Vol. 5, No. 4. October, 1970. Pp. 479–98.

Shulewitz, Malka Hillel. "The B'nei Israel versus the Rabbinate." *Jewish Frontier.* Vol. XXX, No. 8. October 1963. Pp. 7–11.

Siegel, Judy. "Religion and Politics in Israel." *Jerusalem Post.* September 9, 1975. P. 9.

Soifer, Zvi. "Who Is A Jew?" *Israel Digest.* Vol. XVII, No. 21. October 11, 1974. P. 7.

Super, Arthur Saul. "Who is a Jew?" *Jewish Frontier.* Vol. XXVI, No. 3. March, 1959. Pp. 6–10.

Talmon, Jacob Leib. "Who Is A Jew? Letter from Israel." *Encounter.* Vol. XXIV, No. 5. May 1965. Pp. 28–36.

Terlo, Zvi. "The Immigration Laws of Israel—Some Problems." *Public Administration in Israel and Abroad 1965.* Jerusalem. Israel Institute of Public Administration. 1966. Vol. 6. Pp. 31–51.

Weiler, Moses Cyrus. "Who Is A Jew?" *Reconstructionist.* Vol. XXXVII, No. 4. April 2, 1971. Pp. 7–17.

Weisbord, Robert G. "Israel and the Black Hebrew Israelites." *Judaism.* Vol. 24, No. 1. Winter 1975. Pp. 23–38.

"Who Is a Jew?" *ADL Bulletin.* Anti-Defamation League of B'nai B'rith. February, 1970. Pp. 1–2.

Zwergbaum, Aaron. "The Civil Marriage Controversy in Israel." *Congress bi-Weekly.* Vol. 30, No. 15. November 4, 1963. Pp. 18–20.

Table of Cases

Glossary and Pronunciation Guide

The Hebrew language pronunciation officially adopted by the State of Israel is called "Sephardit" (Sfar-dit') and is the pronunciation prevalent among Jews of Spanish and Portuguese ancestry. All the sounds, with one exception, are present in the English language. The exception is the "ch," a sound always pronounced like the German "ch" in "Bach" but a bit softer and less gutteral. It is never sounded like the English "ch" as in "child." However, it is frequently spelled in English with an "h" rather than "ch." Words of more than one syllable are most often accented on the last syllable. Otherwise, the next to the last syllable is generally accented.

Agudat Israel (Ah-goo-daht' Yis-rah-el'), proper noun: Association of Israel, an ultra-Orthodox Jewish religious political party in Israel.

Aguna (Ah-goo-nah'), singular noun: literally "a woman who is shut off"; a wife separated from her husband who has vanished or deserted her and has not communicated with her, thereby preventing her from remarrying until she has proof of his death.

Agunot (Ah-goo-nut'), plural of Aguna.

Aliyah (Ah-lee-yah'), singular noun: literally "ascent" or "going up"; wave of Jewish immigration to Palestine before May 14, 1948 and to Israel after statehood; and also the immigration of an individual Jew to Israel.

Ashkenazi (Ahsh-kuh-nah-zee'), adjective and singular proper noun: derived from the Hebrew word "Ashkenaz" for Germany; a Jew whose origin is Northern, Central or Eastern Europe, particularly Germany or France.

Ashkenazim (Ahsh-kuh-nah-zeem'), plural of Ashkenazi.

Beit Israel (Bayt' Yis-rah-el'), proper noun: literally "House of Israel"; organization of Falashas who left Ethiopia and settled in Israel who maintain they are direct descendants of the ancient Israelite tribe of Dan.

Bene Israel (Beh-nay' Yis-rah-el'), proper noun: literally "Children of Israel"; a sect of Black Jews from India who settled in Israel and who trace their origin to a group of Jewish families that had fled ancient Israel to escape the invading forces of King Antiochus IV in the second century B.C.E

Chalitza (Chah-lee-tzah'), singular noun: a religious ceremony freeing a male from the obligation of marrying the widow of his childless brother. The word literally means "untying" and involves taking off the brother-in-law's shoe by the widow.

Geht (Get), singular noun: a Jewish bill of divorce given by the husband to his wife in the presence of witnesses and requiring the sanction and supervision of a Jewish religious court.

Gemorah (Geh-muh' rah), proper noun: derived from the Aramaic meaning "completion"; the name describing the second part of the Talmud consisting of discussions and commentaries on the first part, the Mishnah.

Ger (Gehr), singular noun: literally "stranger"; a convert to Judaism.

Gerim (Gay-reem'), plural of Ger.

Halachah (Hah-lah-chah'), singular noun: literally "the way," "the path," or "the law"; broadly used to denote the traditional Orthodox Jewish religious law.

Herut (Chay-root'), proper noun: literally "freedom"; the name of a secular rightist political party in Israel which joined with the General Zionist Party in 1965 to form the Gahal bloc.

Histadrut (Hiss-tahd-root'), proper noun: the General Federation of Labor, Israel's largest federation of unions.

Kashruth (Kah-shroot'), noun: literally "fitness"; term describing the Orthodox Jewish religious requirements for ritually fit foods that persons and things must meet.

Kethubah (Keh-too' bah), singular noun: literally "written document"; the marriage contract containing the mutual obligations of wife and husband and given to the bride.

Knesset (Knehs' set), proper noun: literally "assembly," "community," or "congregation"; the Hebrew name for Israel's parliament. Historically, this was the name of the Great Assembly, the Ecclesia or Synagoga Magna, which was the supreme parliamentary authority under Ezra and Nehemia in the fourth and fifth centuries B.C.E.

Kohanim (Ko-hah-neem'), plural noun: literally "priests"; descendants of the priestly class derived from Aaron, the brother of Moses. Jews named "Cohen" are presumed to be "kohanim."

Kosher (Kah-shehr'), adjective: describes foods which are ritually fit to be eaten according to traditional Orthodox Jewish religious law.

Le'um (Lih-oom'), singular noun: Hebrew word for nationality, meaning ethnic affiliation, not citizenship.

Mamzer (Mom' zehr), singular noun: the child born of a union forbidden by traditional Orthodox Jewish religious law.

Mamzerim (Mom-zeh'reem), plural of Mamzer.

Mapai (Mah-pie'), proper noun: initials of Mifleget Poalei Eretz Yisroel (Mih-fleh'get Poh-ah-lay' Eh'retz Yis-rah-el'), Party of the Workers of the Land of Israel, a moderate, democratic socialist political party in Israel, which has been the leading party in all government coalitions since statehood.

Mikveh (Mik'veh), noun: literally "a gathering of waters"; denotes in traditional Orthodox Jewish religious law a special gathering of water obtained from a natural spring, rain or melted natural ice in a pool or bath for ritual immersion to cleanse persons or utensils of ritual impurity.

Mishnah (Mish'nah), proper noun: literally "teaching"; a textbook-like collection recording the Jewish oral law consisting of six sections or orders presenting and discussing the laws on agriculture, festivals and feasts, women with regard to marriage and divorce, civil and criminal law, religious services, and ritual purity and impurity.

Nashim (Nah-sheem'), proper noun: literally "women"; the title of a section or order of the Mishnah dealing with marriage, divorce and vows.

Niddah (Nee'dah), proper noun: literally "menstruation"; a treatise in the sixth order of the Mishnah on the laws of ritual purity and impurity dealing with ritual uncleanliness of women during menstruation or resulting from childbirth and with the regulations governing the ritual cleansing and purification procedures.

Oleh (Oh-leh'), singular noun: literally "one who ascends"; a Jewish immigrant to Israel.

Olim (Oh-leem'), plural of Oleh.

Piskei-Din (Pihs-kay' Deen), proper noun: Law Reports of the Supreme Court of Israel issued by the Ministry of Justice containing the judgments of the Court.

Sephardi (Sfar-dee'), adjective and proper noun: derived from the Hebrew word "Sepharad" (Sfuh-rod') for Spain; a Jew descended from members of the Jewish community of Spain or Portugal driven out by the Inquisitions, particularly of the fifteenth century. The word today describes the Jews who resided thereafter in the Mediterranean countries, North Africa and the Middle East.

Sephardim (Sfar-deem'), plural of Sephardi.

Talmud (Tahl-mood'), proper noun: literally "teaching"; the body of traditional Orthodox Jewish civil and canonical law with rabbinically approved commentaries. It is a term describing the combination of Mishnah and Gemorah and applies to the two Talmudic compilations, the Palestinian and Babylonian Talmuds.

Tehvilah (Teh-vee'lah), noun: literally "immersion"; ritual immersion in a ritual bath (mikveh) for purposes of ritual purity required in order to participate in certain religious ceremonies.

Tohoroth (Tuh-hah-rut'), proper noun: literally "purities"; the sixth order of the Mishnah dealing with ritual impurities and the procedures for purification.

Torah (Tuh-rah'), proper noun: literally "teaching" or "guidance"; technically the first five Books of the Old Testament collectively, or the Pentateuch, but broadly and comprehensively the entire body of Jewish law, both written and oral.

Index